10 Minute Guide to Lotus® 1-2-3® Release 2.4

Katherine Murray
Doug Sabotin
Revised by Hilary J. Adams

A Division of Prentice Hall Computer Publishing
11711 North College, Carmel, Indiana 46032 USA

©1992 by Sams

All rights reserved. No part of this book shall be reproduced, stored in a retrieval system, or transmitted by any means, electronic, mechanical, photocopying, recording, or otherwise, without written permission from the publisher. No patent liability is assumed with respect to the use of the information contained herein. While every precaution has been taken in the preparation of this book, the publisher and authors assume no responsibility for errors or omissions. Neither is any liability assumed for damages resulting from the use of the information contained herein. For information, address Sams, 11711 N. College Ave., Carmel, IN 46032.

International Standard Book Number: 0-672-30117-2
Library of Congress Catalog Card Number: 92-60387

95 94 93 92   8 7 6 5 4 2 1

Interpretation of the printing code: the rightmost double-digit number is the year of the book's first printing; the rightmost single-digit number is the number of the book's printing. For example, a printing code of 92-1 shows that this copy of the book was printed during the first printing of the book in 1992.

Publisher: *Richard K. Swadley*
Associate Publisher: *Marie Butler-Knight*
Managing Editor: *Elizabeth Keaffaber*
Product Development Manager: *Lisa Bucki*
Acquisitions Editor: *Stephen Poland*
Development Editor: *Faithe Wempen*
Production Editor: *Linda Hawkins*
Manuscript Editor: *Howard Peirce*
Cover Design: *Dan Armstrong*
Designer: *Michele Laseau*
Production Team: *Brook Farling, Joelynn Gifford, Debbie Hanna, Betty Kish, Bob LaRoche, David McKenna, Matthew Morrill, Barry Pruett, Linda Seifert, Kevin Spear, Suzanne Tully, Jeff Valler, Mary Beth Wakefield, Corinne Walls, Jenny Watson, Lisa Wilson*
Indexer: *Tina M. Trettin*

Special thanks to C. Herbert Feltner for assuring the technical accuracy of this book.

Screen reproductions in this book were created by means of the program Collage Plus from Inner Media, Inc., Hollis, NH.

Printed in the United States of America

Contents

Introduction, vii

1 Starting Lotus 1-2-3, 1
Starting 1-2-3, 1
What If 1-2-3 Doesn't Start?, 2
Turning on Wysiwyg, 3

2 Exploring the Lotus 1-2-3 Screen, 4
Elements of the 1-2-3 Screen, 4
Using the Keyboard, 9
Using the Mouse, 10

3 Using Menus and Dialog Boxes, 11
Introducing the Main Menu, 11
Opening the Main Menu, 12
Selecting a Command, 13
Entering Information After Selecting a Command, 14
Using Dialog Boxes, 16

4 Using SmartIcons, 18
What Are SmartIcons?, 18
Using SmartIcons, 19
Adding Icons to the Custom Palette, 20
Removing Icons from the Custom Palette, 21

5   Entering Data, 22

Planning the Worksheet, 22
Entering Labels, 23
Entering Values, 25

6   Saving the Worksheet and Exiting 1-2-3, 27

Saving the Worksheet, 27
Saving a New Worksheet, 28
Saving a Modified Worksheet, 30
Exiting 1-2-3, 31

7   Retrieving a Worksheet, 32

Retrieving a Worksheet, 32
Displaying a List of Files, 33
Undoing the Retrieve, 34

8   Using 1-2-3's Add-In Programs, 36

What Are Add-Ins?, 36
Attaching Add-Ins, 37
Invoking Add-Ins, 38
Using the Viewer Add-In, 39
Removing an Add-In, 40

9   Working with Ranges, 41

Why Use Ranges?, 41
Selecting a Range, 42
Naming Ranges, 45
Deleting Range Names and Erasing Ranges, 47

10   Using Formulas and Functions, 49

What Is a Formula?, 49
Entering a Formula, 50
Editing a Formula, 54
Displaying Formulas, 54
Using the Auditor, 55

11   Copying and Moving Cells, 58

Understanding Relative and Absolute Cell Referencing, 58
Copying Cells, 60
Moving Cells, 62

12 Editing and Deleting Cells, 64
Editing Cells, 64
Setting Recalculation, 66
Deleting Cells, 67

13 Formatting the Worksheet, 69
Formatting Ranges, 69
Formatting the Entire Worksheet, 72

14 Formatting: Changing Column Width, 74
Changing Individual Column Width, 75
Changing the Width of All Columns, 76
Resetting Column Width, 78
Hiding Columns, 78
Redisplaying Columns, 80

15 Formatting: Aligning Labels, 81
Understanding Label Alignment, 81
Repeating Labels, 84

16 Working with Rows and Columns, 86
Adding Rows and Columns, 86
Deleting Rows and Columns, 88

17 Using Wysiwyg, 89
What Is Wysiwyg?, 89
Attaching Wysiwyg, 89
Changing the Appearance of Text, 91

18 Printing Worksheets, 97
Starting the Print Operation, 97
Printing a Screen, 100
Adding Headers and Footers, 100
Printing Worksheet Formulas, 102

19 Creating a Basic Graph, 103
Understanding Graph Types, 103
Creating a Bar Graph, 104
Creating a Pie Graph, 107

20 Enhancing Graphs, 109

Enhancing the Graph, 109
Adding Titles, 109
Adding a Legend, 111
Setting a Background Grid, 112
Naming a Graph, 113
Saving a Graph, 114

21 Printing a Graph, 115

Starting PrintGraph, 115
The PrintGraph Menu, 116
Getting Ready to Print, 117
Printing a Simple Graph, 118
Enhancing the Printout, 118

22 Creating a Simple Database, 121

What Is a Database?, 121
Understanding the 1-2-3 Database, 121
Building the Database, 123

23 Sorting a Database, 125

Understanding 1-2-3 Sort Operations, 125
Sorting on One Key Field, 126
Sorting on Two Key Fields, 129

24 Searching for Data   132

Understanding Search Operations, 132
Determining the Criteria Range, 133
Extracting Records, 136

Table of Functions, 139

Table of Features, 141

SmartIcons, 144

DOS Primer, 149

Index, 159

Introduction

Perhaps you walked into work this morning and found a Lotus 1-2-3 Release 2.4 package sitting beside your computer, along with a new mouse. Until now, all you've heard about 1-2-3 is that it allows users to create spreadsheets for performing calculations and graphs for displaying numeric data as effectively as possible. A few things are certain. You need:

- To navigate 1-2-3 quickly and easily.

- To identify and learn the tasks necessary to accomplish your particular needs.

- Some clear-cut, plain-English help to learn the basic features of the program.

Welcome to the *10 Minute Guide to Lotus 1-2-3 Release 2.4*. Because most people don't have the luxury of sitting down uninterrupted for hours at a time to learn a new program, the *10 Minute Guide* teaches the operations you need in lessons that you can complete in 10 minutes or less. The 10-minute format offers information in bite-sized, easy-to-follow modules; it lets you stop and start as often as you like because each lesson is a self-contained series of steps.

Conventions Used in This Book

The following icons help you find your way around the *10 Minute Guide to Lotus 1-2-3 Release 2.4:*

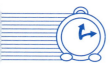 **Timesaver Tips** These offer shortcuts and hints for using the program more effectively.

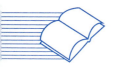 **Plain English** Look here for definitions of new terms.

 **Panic Buttons** These point out problem areas—how to identify them and how to solve them.

 SmartIcons Identify information about this new feature and ways it can make your work easier.

A Table of Features, a Table of Functions, and a list of SmartIcons at the end of the book provide you with a quick guide to 1-2-3 features not covered fully in this book. The DOS Primer introduces often-used DOS commands and procedures.

Specific conventions are used to help you find your way around 1-2-3 as easily as possible:

| Numbered steps | Step-by-step instructions are highlighted so that you can easily find the procedures you need to perform basic 1-2-3 operations. |

Introduction

`On-screen text`	On-screen text will appear in a special monospace font.
What you type	Information you type will appear in a bold, color, monospace font.
Items you select	Items you select or keys you press will appear in color.
Menu names	The names of menus, commands, buttons and dialog boxes are shown with the first letter capitalized for easy recognition.

What's New with Release 2.4?

Lotus 1-2-3 Release 2.4 offers features that earlier versions of 1-2-3 did not possess. These new enhancements include:

- SmartIcons that allow you to perform common 1-2-3 operations with a single mouse click or a few keystrokes (see Lesson 4 and SmartIcon tips in all the lessons).

- BackSolver, an add-in program that allows you to determine a result for a group of formulas and have 1-2-3 calculate the values needed to get that result.

- SmartPics, a collection of ready-made graphic objects (in CGM format) for use in 1-2-3 worksheets.

- Landscape printing support for all printers, including dot-matrix.

- Importing and printing Encapsulated PostScript (EPS) files.

- Use of the Translate utility to convert a 1-2-3 Release 2.x file (WK1) to a 1-2-3 Release 3.x file (WK3), along with conversion of corresponding FMT files to FM3 files.

For Further Reference, Consult . . .

The First Book of Lotus 1-2-3 Release 2.4 by Alan Simpson and Paul Lichtman (from Sams), revised by Jennifer Flynn.

Trademarks

All terms mentioned in this book that are known to be trademarks or service marks are listed below. In addition, terms suspected of being trademarks or service marks have been appropriately capitalized. Sams cannot attest to the accuracy of this information. Use of a term in this book should not be regarded as affecting the validity of any trademark or service mark.

Lotus and 1-2-3 are registered trademarks of Lotus Development Corporation.

MS-DOS is a registered trademark of Microsoft Corporation.

Lesson 1
Starting Lotus 1-2-3

In this lesson you'll learn how to start Lotus 1-2-3.

Before you begin working in Lotus 1-2-3, you must have already installed the program on your hard disk. Make sure that you have installed it correctly. The 1-2-3 installation program asks for information about your monitor, printer, and any other devices associated with your computer. Providing the correct information will allow you to work more efficiently in 1-2-3. (See the inside front cover for installation instructions.)

Starting 1-2-3

To start 1-2-3 from your hard disk, follow these steps:

1. Make sure the DOS prompt displays the drive on which you have installed 1-2-3. This will usually be either C: or D:.

2. To get to the 1-2-3 Release 2.4 directory, type **CD\123R24** and press Enter. This directory is where you installed the 1-2-3 program information.

3. Type **123** and press Enter. You will see a copyright screen for a brief moment, and then the work area will appear, as shown in Figure 1.1.

Lesson 1

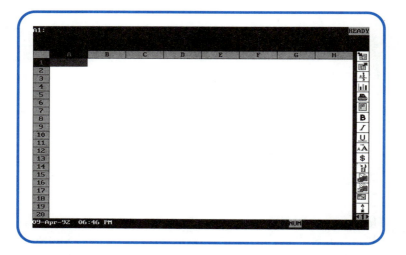

Figure 1.1 The initial work area in 1-2-3.

What If 1-2-3 Doesn't Start?

In most cases, 1-2-3 will start without any problem. There is a chance, however, that after you follow the previous steps, 1-2-3 will not start. If this happens, you will see an error message such as Bad command or filename.

Before you go back to the installation process, make sure that you have followed the steps correctly. If so, try the steps again. If you get the same error message, 1-2-3 may not be installed correctly; refer to the inside front cover of this book for installation instructions.

Turning on Wysiwyg

Wysiwyg (what-you-see-is-what-you-get) is a display mode in which your input looks approximately the same on-screen as it will when printed. All the figures in this book were created with 1-2-3 in Wysiwyg mode.

If you have an appropriate video card and monitor, 1-2-3 Release 2.4 should start up in Wysiwyg mode automatically. If it does not, follow these steps to attach Wysiwyg.

1. Press / (slash) to activate 1-2-3's Main menu, or move the mouse pointer to the blank area above the worksheet (called the *control panel* or *menu area*).

2. Use the arrow keys or the mouse to select Add-in.

3. Select Attach.

4. Select WYSIWYG.ADN from the list of add-ins displayed. (Press → to view additional choices if needed.)

5. Press Enter twice.

6. Select Quit to return to READY mode.

For more information about Wysiwyg and other add-in programs, see Lesson 8.

In this lesson you learned how to start Lotus 1-2-3. In the next lesson you'll explore the 1-2-3 work area.

Lesson 2
Exploring the Lotus 1-2-3 Screen

In this lesson you'll learn about the basic elements of the Lotus 1-2-3 screen.

Elements of the 1-2-3 Screen

The 1-2-3 screen contains all the elements—menus, commands, work area, and mode indicators—you need in order to work with 1-2-3. Figure 2.1 shows a typical 1-2-3 screen. You can display this screen by pressing the slash key (/) or moving the mouse pointer into the menu area.

The Work Area

The work area is perhaps the most obvious screen element. Organized in columns and rows like a sheet of columnar paper from an accountant's pad, the work area helps you organize and work with the data in your worksheets.

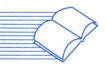

Cell In any spreadsheet program, a *cell* is the intersection of one column and one row. For example, cell C6 is the intersection of column C and row 6.

Exploring the Lotus 1-2-3 Screen

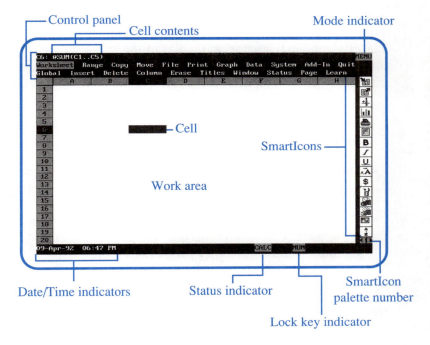

Figure 2.1 The 1-2-3 screen.

Across the top of the work area you see a highlighted line that helps you identify the column the cursor is in. There are 256 columns, lettered from A to IV. The left edge of the work area is bordered by another highlighted line numbering the rows of the worksheet from 1 to 8,192.

Reading Cell Addresses When you are referring to a cell, you list the column first and then the row. For example, if you are referring to the fourth cell in column E, you would write that cell address as **E4**.

Although the spreadsheet extends all the way to IV8192, only cells A1 through H20 are shown on the initial screen.

5

Lesson 2

The Control Panel

The control panel appears at the top of the 1-2-3 screen. In the control panel, you choose menus and commands to interact with 1-2-3. The control panel contains three lines:

- The first line gives information about the currently highlighted cell.

- The second line shows the characters being entered or edited or, when menus are activated, shows the menu.

- The third line provides a description of the command being used or, when menus are active, lists the options available for the currently highlighted command.

Look at the control panel in Figure 2.1. The first line shows the address of the cell and displays the formula that is currently being stored in that cell. The second line shows the Main menu, and the third line shows the options available for the highlighted Worksheet command.

Mode Indicators

The mode indicators appear in the upper right corner of the 1-2-3 screen. Table 2.1 lists the modes available in 1-2-3 and provides a brief description of each.

Table 2.1 Mode indicators.

Mode	Description
EDIT	The contents of a cell are being edited.
ERROR	A formula or operation causes an error; press Esc or Enter to remove the ERROR indicator.

Exploring the Lotus 1-2-3 Screen

Mode	Description
FILES	You need to select a file name.
FIND	A database search operation is being performed.
HELP	A help screen is displayed.
LABEL	You are entering a label.
POINT	You are selecting a range.
NAMES	You need to select a range name from a displayed list.
MENU	You are selecting a menu option.
READY	The program is waiting for a cell entry or command.
VALUE	You are entering a number or formula.
WAIT	1-2-3 is processing a command.
SETTINGS	You have activated a dialog box.
STAT	You are displaying a STATUS screen.

Lock Key Indicators

The lock key indicators are displayed in the lower right corner of the screen. Most keyboards have lock keys—such as Scroll Lock, Num Lock, Caps Lock, INS, OVR—which act as toggles; that is, you press the key once to turn on the feature and press the key again to turn it off.

Status Indicators

The last type of indicators used by the 1-2-3 spreadsheet are status indicators. These indicators tell you the type of operation 1-2-3 is performing, or let you know when an error has occurred, as well as what type of error it is (see Table 2.2).

Removing Error Messages To remove a status indicator error and return the spreadsheet to READY mode, press Esc or Enter.

Table 2.2 Status indicators.

Indicator	Description
CALC	The worksheet needs to be recalculated.
CIRC	There is a circular reference error.
CMD	A macro or Command Language program is running.
MEM	1-2-3 is running out of RAM to load a program or manipulate a worksheet.
SST	A macro or Command Language program is running in step-by-step mode.
STEP	You are stepping through a macro or Command Language program.
UNDO	Indicates that Undo feature is active.
LEARN	A macro is being recorded from your keystrokes.

Exploring the Lotus 1-2-3 Screen

Using the Keyboard

Now that you know the basics of the 1-2-3 screen, you need to know how to use the keyboard to move around the display. Table 2.3 lists the keys you'll use to move the cursor (also called the cell pointer) in the worksheet area.

Table 2.3   Keys for moving the cursor.

Key	Function
↓	Moves the cursor down one row.
↑	Moves the cursor up one row.
→	Moves the cursor right one cell or to the next command or option.
←	Moves the cursor left one cell or to the previous command or option.
Tab	Moves the cursor right one screen.
Shift-Tab	Moves the cursor left one screen.

Starting with A1 as the active cell, try the following examples:

1. Press ↓ four times. (The cursor moves to cell A5.)

2. Press → twice. (The cursor moves to C5.)

3. Press Tab. (The entire display is scrolled to the right one screen. The cursor is positioned in cell I5.)

4. Press Shift-Tab. (The display is returned to the earlier display, with the cursor in cell A5.)

Lesson 2

Using the Mouse

Lotus 1-2-3 allows you to use a mouse as well as the keyboard. Following are a few terms you should be familiar with if you are using a mouse:

Point Move the mouse until the cell or menu option you want is highlighted.

Click When you have highlighted the cell or option you want, press and release the mouse button.

Drag Position the mouse at the point you want to begin highlighting; then press and hold the mouse button while you move the mouse to highlight the entire group of cells you want to select.

To select menu options with the mouse:

1. Display the Main menu by moving the mouse pointer from the worksheet into the control panel.

2. Point to the menu option you want to select.

3. Click the mouse button.

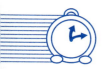

Getting Help You can get help by pressing F1 to display the 1-2-3 Main Help Index. Choose a topic using the arrow keys or by clicking it with the mouse.

Click on the Help SmartIcon from icon palette 4 to see 1-2-3's main help screen. Using the keyboard, press Alt-F7 and use ↑ or ↓ to highlight the Help SmartIcon, and then press Enter.

Lesson 3
Using Menus and Dialog Boxes

In this lesson you'll learn how to use the menu system and dialog boxes in Lotus 1-2-3.

Introducing the Main Menu

The Main menu contains the commands you'll use as you work in 1-2-3. Table 3.1 explains them.

Table 3.1 Commands in the Main menu.

Command	Description
Worksheet	Contains the commands that affect the entire worksheet.
Range	Includes commands used to select and work with a range of cells.
Copy	Enables you to copy a cell or range of cells.
Move	Enables you to move a cell or range of cells.
File	Allows you to perform various file-maintenance operations.
Print	Enables you to print a range or an entire worksheet.
Graph	Helps you choose settings for a graph that you create or modify.

continues

Lesson 3

Table 3.1 Continued.

Command	Description
Data	Allows you to work with the database features of 1-2-3.
System	Temporarily exits 1-2-3 and opens the operating system.
Add-in	Enables you to work with add-in programs.
Quit	Ends the current work session.

Opening the Main Menu

Before you can use the menu, you first must open it. To do this, follow these steps:

1. Make sure that the worksheet you are working on is in READY mode. The word READY should appear in the top right corner of the screen. (Press Esc to clear any other mode.)

2. Press the / (slash) key or move the mouse pointer into the menu area to open the Main menu in the control panel (see Figure 3.1).

Using the Slash Key Don't confuse the / (slash) key with the \ (backslash) key. If you press \ (backslash) by mistake, press Esc and you will return to the original screen; then press / (slash) and the menu will appear.

Using Menus and Dialog Boxes

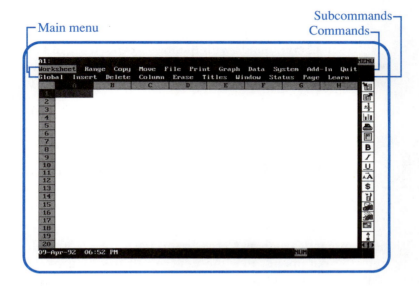

Figure 3.1 The Main menu in the control panel.

Figure 3.1 shows the commands available in the Main menu. The second line of commands lists the subcommands available after you select a command on the first line. As you move the highlight from command to command, the second line changes to show you the additional commands that are available.

Selecting a Command

To move through and select a command in the Main menu with the keyboard, use the following steps:

1. After you open the Main menu, use ← and → to move through the list until the command you need is highlighted.

Lesson 3

2. Press Enter.

To select commands with the mouse, move the mouse pointer into the control panel area of the screen. When the Main menu appears, click on the command you want to activate.

Selecting a Command You can choose a command from the Main menu quickly by pressing the first letter of the command you want or by clicking on it with the mouse.

A few of the commands in the Main menu do not have subcommands, such as Copy. In this case, after you highlight the command, the line underneath the Main menu displays a description of what the command will do if selected.

What If I Select the Wrong Command? If you accidentally choose the wrong command or subcommand, press Esc on the keyboard. 1-2-3 will take you back to the previous step.

Entering Information After Selecting a Command

In some instances, after you select a command you must type information that will allow you to continue. Try the following example:

1. From the Main menu, move the highlight to the File menu name.

2. Press Enter or click the left mouse button.

3. Highlight the Save command, which is used to save a worksheet you've created.

4. Press Enter or click the left mouse button. You will be shown a list of all the files currently saved in 1-2-3. Assume the worksheet you have created is a new one.

5. Press Esc. You will see the following message in the control panel: Enter name of file to save:.

6. Use the appropriate keys to delete and type the appropriate path and file name for the worksheet. (Just type a name; don't bother with an extension.)

7. Press Enter or click the left mouse button.

8. To return to the Main menu, press Esc repeatedly until the Main menu appears on-screen.

Path refers to the drive and directory where the file will be stored. For more information see your DOS manual.

A **file extension** is an addition to the file name that helps identify the type of file. The file extension is separated from the main part of the name by a period (for example, in TEST.WK1, WK1 is the extension). You don't have to worry about assigning extensions, because 1-2-3 does it automatically.

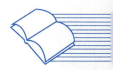

Lesson 3

Using Dialog Boxes

Dialog boxes pop up over your worksheet to show you a set of options available for the operation you are performing. For example, Figure 3.2 shows a dialog box displayed when you select /Worksheet Global.

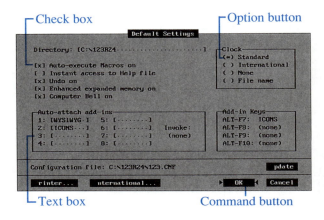

Figure 3.2 An example of a dialog box.

Dialog Box Elements

Dialog boxes contain several different elements that help you make selections. Table 3.2 lists the various elements and provides a brief description of each.

Using Menus and Dialog Boxes

Table 3.2   Dialog box elements.

Element	Description
Option buttons	Use to select individual settings (as in the Recalculation column, Natural).
Check boxes	Use to select one or more items in a list of options.
Text boxes	Use to type a specific setting.
List boxes	Use to choose from a list of displayed options.
Command buttons	Use to carry out the dialog box operation (usually OK or Cancel).

Making Dialog Box Selections

When you want to select an item in a dialog box, follow these steps using the keyboard:

1. Press F2 to enter EDIT mode.

2. Press Tab until the option group you want is highlighted or press the first letter in the name of the option group.

3. Use the arrow keys to move the highlight to the option you want.

4. Press the space bar to select the item.

Lesson 4
Using SmartIcons

In this lesson you'll learn to use 1-2-3's SmartIcons.

What Are SmartIcons?

SmartIcons appear in a column on the right side of your screen. They provide quick, easy access to 1-2-3 commands and macros. When you select a SmartIcon, you're really performing a 1-2-3 command. For example, when you select the Save SmartIcon, you're using the /File Save command without going through 1-2-3's menus.

1-2-3 provides 77 SmartIcons arranged into six palettes, plus one palette you can customize to include the icons you use most often. An example of a SmartIcon palette is shown in Figure 4.1.

Where Are They? If you don't see icons like those in Figure 4.1, make sure that both the Icons add-in and Wysiwyg are attached. See Lesson 8 for information on attaching add-ins.

Using SmartIcons

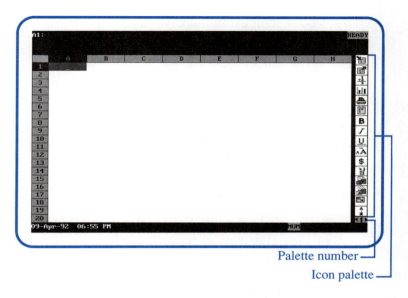

Figure 4.1 A sample SmartIcon palette.

Using SmartIcons

SmartIcons are arranged into palettes. The number of each palette is displayed at the bottom of the column of icons (see Figure 4.1). Icon palette 1 is the custom palette—you can add or remove icons to suit your needs. The other icon palettes can't be modified. A complete list of SmartIcons and their functions is provided in the back of this book.

To select a SmartIcon using the mouse, click on it. Click on the arrow to either side of the palette number to scroll through the available palettes.

19

Lesson 4

To select an icon using the keyboard:

1. In READY mode, press Alt-F7.

2. Press ← or → to select the palette.

3. Press ↑ or ↓ to move the highlight to the icon you want to use. Use the Home and End keys to move to the first and last icons on the palette.

4. Press Enter to activate the SmartIcon.

Nothing Happens!   Some SmartIcons (Copy and Move, for example) operate only on ranges of data. You must select the range before you select the SmartIcon.

Adding Icons to the Custom Palette

The custom palette is palette 1, the default palette that appears when you start 1-2-3. You can have up to 16 icons on your custom palette at one time. If you add an icon when the palette is full, 1-2-3 replaces the bottom icon on the palette. (Later in this lesson you'll learn to remove a specific icon from the palette.) To add an icon to the custom palette, follow these steps:

1. Select icon palette 6.

2. Select the Add Icon SmartIcon. (It looks like a stack of icons with a plus (+) sign.)

3. Select the icon you want to add to the custom palette. If you're using a mouse, click on the desired icon. If you're using the keyboard, highlight it and press Enter.

1-2-3 replaces the last icon on the custom palette and returns you to READY mode. To add more icons, repeat the process.

Icons added to the custom palette do not disappear from their home palette. The icon isn't moved—it is copied. Similarly, icons removed from the custom palette are not removed from their home palettes.

Removing Icons from the Custom Palette

To remove an icon from your custom palette:

1. Select icon palette 6.

2. Select the Del Icon SmartIcon. 1-2-3 will display the custom icon palette.

3. Select the icon you want to remove from the palette. (Click on it, or highlight it with the arrow keys and press Enter.) 1-2-3 deletes the icon.

Help on SmartIcons To see a description of a SmartIcon before you use it, press Alt-F7 and highlight the icon. If you're using the mouse, click on the icon with the right mouse button. 1-2-3 displays a description of the icon in line three of the control panel.

In this lesson you learned how to customize a SmartIcon palette by adding and removing icons. In the next lesson you'll learn how to enter data into your worksheets.

Lesson 5
Entering Data

In this lesson you'll enter data and begin creating your worksheet.

Planning the Worksheet

Before you begin creating worksheets on your own, you'll want to consider what type of data you'll be working with. Think about the information and decide which data should be placed in columns and which should be placed in rows.

For example, suppose you are the owner of ABC Bakery, and you want to find out which of your products makes the most money. For a three-month period, you could keep separate totals for your catering, walk-in, and special-order customers. At the end of that time, you could use 1-2-3 to analyze the results.

In planning your worksheet, you realize that each of the three months—January, February, and March—should occupy a column, and the three totals—Catering, Walk-In, and Special Order—should occupy rows. Figure 5.1 shows the completed worksheet.

Entering Data

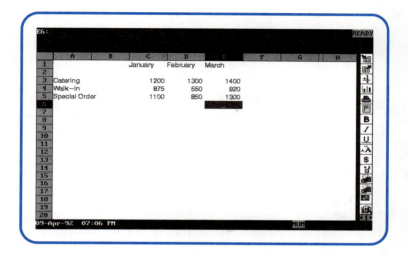

Figure 5.1 The sample worksheet.

Entering Labels

After you've decided how you want to organize the worksheet, you need to enter labels. (You cannot enter data when the Main menu is displayed, however. If the Main menu is showing, press Esc to return to the worksheet.) For most worksheets, you'll want to enter both column and row labels. For this example, do the column labels first.

Adding Column Labels

To add column labels, type the label and press → after each entry. For example, follow these steps:

1. Starting in cell A1, press → twice to move to cell C1.

2. In C1, type **January**. Press →.

23

Lesson 5

3. In D1, type **February**. Press → again.

4. In E1, type **March**. Press →.

Use the Enter Key When entering data in a row, you may find it easier to use the Enter key after each entry. Pressing Enter accepts the entry.

Adding Row Labels

Row labels extend down a column of the worksheet (usually the first column, A). To add row labels, type the label and press ↓ after each entry. For example, follow these steps:

1. Start in cell A1. Press ↓ twice to move to cell A3.

2. In A3, type **Catering**. Press ↓.

3. In A4, type **Walk-In**. Press ↓.

4. In A5, type **Special Order**. Press ↓.

Figure 5.2 shows the worksheet with the column and row labels entered.

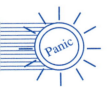

Lengthy Labels If you enter a label that is longer than the column is wide, 1-2-3 displays the label by using part of the next cell if no information is currently entered in that cell. You may want to change the width of the column to display the entire label without intruding on subsequent cells. (Lesson 14 explains how to change column width.)

Entering Data

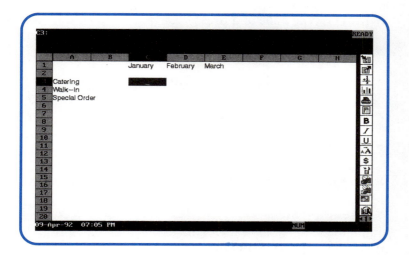

Figure 5.2 The labels in the worksheet.

Aligning Labels By default, labels are left-aligned. 1-2-3 also gives you the options of centering or right-aligning labels. Lesson 15 explains more about working with the label format.

Entering Values

After you enter the labels in the worksheet, you're ready to enter the values. Use the same technique you used for entering labels. Type the entry and then use an arrow key to accept your entry and move to another cell. For example, follow these steps:

1. Use the arrow keys to move the cell pointer to cell C3.

2. In C3, type **1200** and press →.

25

Lesson 5 ───────────────────────────────

3. In D3, type **1300** and press →.

4. In E3, type **1400** and press ↓.

5. Press ← twice to move the cell pointer back to cell C4.

6. In C4, type **875** and press →.

7. In D4, type **550** and press →.

8. In E4, type **920** and press ↓.

9. Press ← twice.

10. In C5, type **1100** and press →.

11. In D5, type **850** and press →.

12. In E5, type **1300** and press ↓.

Your sample worksheet should now resemble the one shown in Figure 5.1.

Now you know how to create a basic worksheet. Before you can really analyze anything, of course, you need to be able to perform calculations on the worksheet values. In later lessons you'll learn how to use functions and formulas to work with the data you've entered in this lesson.

In this lesson you learned how to enter labels and data into a worksheet. In the next lesson you'll learn how to save the sample worksheet you've created.

Lesson 6
Saving the Worksheet and Exiting 1-2-3

In this lesson you'll learn how to save your work and exit 1-2-3.

Saving a Worksheet

When you create a worksheet in 1-2-3, the program temporarily holds the work in its memory. After you have finished a work session or have made significant changes to a worksheet, you need to save your work. Saving a worksheet stores it permanently on a floppy or hard disk. This procedure ensures that you can get back to this worksheet in the future if necessary.

There are a few rules you should keep in mind when you save a worksheet. The file name:

- Can be up to eight characters long.

- Can contain letters, numbers, and the underscore (_) or hyphen (-) characters.

- Cannot contain any blank spaces, or any of the following characters: + = / [ ] " : ; ? * \ < > ¦

Lesson 6 ─────────────────────────────

Saving a New Worksheet

To save a newly created worksheet in 1-2-3:

1. Make sure that the program is in READY mode. (The word READY will appear in the top right corner of the screen.)

2. Press / (slash) or move the mouse pointer into the menu area to activate the Main menu.

3. Select File.

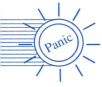

Forget How to Select Commands? There are several ways to select a command. You can type the first letter of its name, use the arrow keys to highlight it and then press Enter, or click on the command with the mouse.

4. Select Save. Line 3 of the control panel shows a horizontal list of the files saved in 1-2-3, similar to the one shown in Figure 6.1.

5. To activate the default file name line so that you can enter your own file name, press Esc. You should see a flashing cursor preceded by the directory that the file will be saved in, as shown in Figure 6.2.

6. If this is the directory you want to save your worksheet in, type the appropriate file name. If not, backspace over the default directory and type in the directory and file name you would like to use. (Name the sample file ABC-A.)

7. Press Enter. The worksheet is then saved.

Saving the Worksheet and Exiting 1-2-3

Worksheet file names

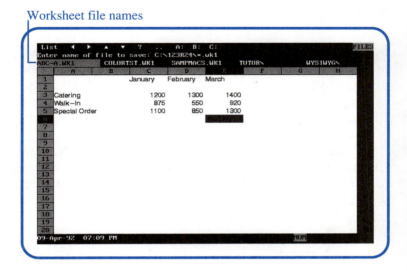

Figure 6.1 The list of files saved in 1-2-3.

Prompt line

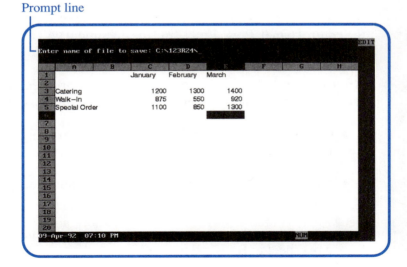

Figure 6.2 Entering the name of the file to save.

Lesson 6

Saving a Modified Worksheet

Sometimes you must modify a file that you have saved previously. In this case, you can save the worksheet in one of two ways: as a new worksheet with a new file name, or as an updated version of the same worksheet (with the same file name).

If you want to save the modified worksheet with a new file name, follow the steps for saving a new worksheet (described in the previous section). To save a worksheet with the file name it was last saved under, follow these steps:

1. From READY mode, press / (slash) to activate the Main menu.

2. Choose File.

3. Select Save. 1-2-3 shows you the existing file name in the control panel. Press Enter, and the document will be saved in its current form.

4. After you press Enter to save the modified worksheet with the same name, you can do one of three things:

    - Cancel the command, which will leave the existing file in memory but not saved on disk.

    - Replace the existing file with the modified version.

    - Backup the new file by giving the old version of the worksheet a .BAK extension.

Saving the Worksheet and Exiting 1-2-3

5. Highlight your choice, and press Enter. This will save your worksheet according to the choice that you have made.

Fast Save To save either a new or modified worksheet quickly, use the Save SmartIcon on icon palette 2.

Exiting 1-2-3

After you have finished working in 1-2-3 and have saved the work you have done, you need to know how to exit 1-2-3. To get back to the DOS prompt, follow these steps:

1. From READY mode, press / (slash) to activate the Main menu.

2. Select Quit. 1-2-3 prompts you to end your 1-2-3 session in the control panel.

3. Choose Yes to end your 1-2-3 session. You will return to the DOS prompt.

Saving Your Work If you have been working in 1-2-3 and have not saved your work, the program gives you one last chance to save it before exiting. To save the worksheet, select No at the prompt to exit 1-2-3, which returns you to the worksheet so that you can save it. You can then exit the program as usual.

Lesson 7
Retrieving a Worksheet

In this lesson you'll learn how to retrieve a saved worksheet.

Retrieving a Worksheet

After working in 1-2-3 for some time, you will accumulate worksheets that you have created and saved throughout your work sessions. You will probably need to go back into each of these files more than once.

Losing the Current Worksheet When you retrieve a worksheet, the new worksheet automatically erases the worksheet on-screen. Make sure that you have saved your current worksheet before you retrieve any other.

To retrieve a worksheet that you have saved, follow these steps:

1. From READY mode, press / (slash) on the keyboard to activate the Main menu.

2. Select File.

3. Choose Retrieve. 1-2-3 displays a horizontal list of the available files, as shown in Figure 7.1.

Retrieving a Worksheet

List indicator

Figure 7.1 The Retrieve command dialog area.

4. Move through the list of files using the arrow keys until the file you need is highlighted. Or, if you know the file name of the worksheet, press Esc and the Name of file to retrieve: prompt will appear. You then can type in the file name or click on it with the mouse.

5. Press Enter.

Displaying a List of Files

Rather than scroll through the horizontal list of file names displayed in the control panel, you can display a full-screen list.

To display a full-screen list, press F3 or click the mouse on the List indicator in the top left corner of the screen (shown in Figure 7.1). The spreadsheet disappears, and you

33

Lesson 7

see a full-screen list of files in the current directory (see Figure 7.2).

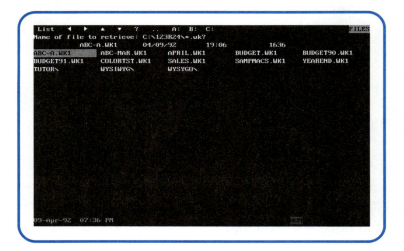

Figure 7.2   Using the List feature to show directory contents.

To select the file you want, click on the name of the file in the displayed list or use the arrow keys to highlight the file you want and then press Enter.

 Click on the Retrieve SmartIcon to display the list of files to retrieve. The Retrieve SmartIcon is on icon palette 5.

Undoing the Retrieve

If you retrieve a saved worksheet and have forgotten to save your previous work or need to get back to it, you can return to the previous worksheet as long as you have not begun working on the retrieved file. To get back to the previous worksheet, follow these steps:

1. Make sure that the UNDO indicator appears in the status line of the work area, as shown in Figure 7.3.

2. Press Alt-F4 to return to the previous worksheet.

If UNDO Isn't Displayed   If UNDO does not appear in the status line, turn the Undo feature on by selecting /Worksheet Global Default Other Undo Enable and then choosing /Worksheet Default Other Update. This won't bring back something that's already been deleted, but will set up protection for the next time.

 To undo operations quickly, click on the Undo SmartIcon in icon palette 4.

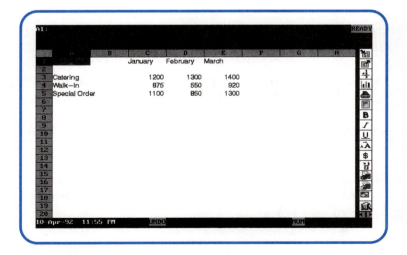

Figure 7.3   The Undo feature in Lotus 1-2-3.

Lesson 8

Using 1-2-3's Add-In Programs

In this lesson you'll find out how to load the add-in programs included with 1-2-3 Release 2.4.

What Are Add-Ins?

An add-in program is a special utility that adds to the capabilities of 1-2-3 while you are using the program. 1-2-3 Release 2.4 includes seven different add-in programs:

- Wysiwyg, a program that allows you to see your spreadsheet on-screen the way it will appear in print.

- Tutorial, a step-by-step program that leads you through the basics of using Release 2.4.

- Spreadsheet Auditor, which allows you to examine and check the formulas in your worksheet.

- Viewer, a program that lets you view the contents of spreadsheet, database, and text files without retrieving them into 1-2-3.

- Macro Library Manager, a feature that stores important items—such as macros, ranges, and formulas—which you use repeatedly in different spreadsheets.

Using 1-2-3's Add-In Programs

- BackSolver, a new program that allows you to solve "what-if" problems.

- Icons, the program which displays SmartIcons. SmartIcons are discussed in Lesson 4.

Attaching Add-Ins

Before you can use one of the add-in programs, you must load the program (this is known as attaching the add-in). To attach an add-in, follow these steps:

1. Press / (slash) to display the Main menu.

2. Select Add-In.

3. Select Attach. 1-2-3 lists the add-ins (see Figure 8.1).

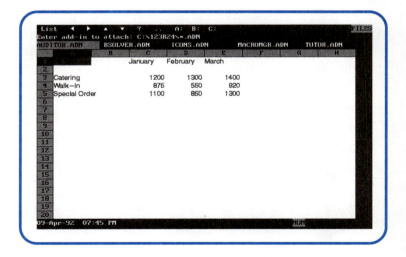

Figure 8.1   Selecting an add-in.

37

Lesson 8

4. Highlight the name of the add-in you want to use. (For example, choose VIEWER.ADN.)

5. Press Enter. 1-2-3 gives you the option of assigning the add-in to a specific key so that you can start the program with a single keystroke. For now, leave No Key highlighted.

6. Press Enter again. 1-2-3 attaches the add-in so that you can use it as necessary. Select Quit to return to READY mode.

Out of Memory? If 1-2-3 tells you that the needed memory is in use, detach one of the other add-ins before loading the desired add-in. (Detaching is discussed later in this lesson.)

Invoking Add-Ins

When you are ready to use the add-in program you've selected, you need to use the /Add-In Invoke command to start the program. Try the following example:

1. Press / (slash) to display the Main menu.

2. Select Add-In.

3. Select Invoke.

4. Choose the add-in from the list of available add-in programs. (For example, choose VIEWER.)

5. Press Enter. The add-in is now ready to use.

Using 1-2-3's Add-In Programs

Using the Viewer Add-In

To illustrate how to use an add-in, consider Viewer as an example. Viewer allows you to look at the contents of a file without actually retrieving the file into your worksheet. First, attach and invoke Viewer, if you haven't already done so, using the steps in the preceding sections. When the Viewer screen is displayed, you can Retrieve, Link, or Browse through files within Viewer (see Figure 8.2).

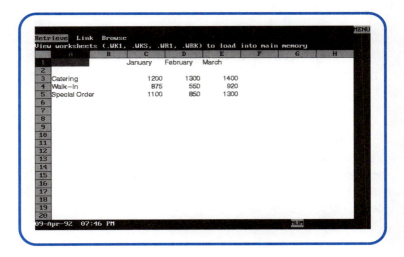

Figure 8.2   Selecting Viewer options.

To display the Viewer screen, select Retrieve. The screen shown in Figure 8.3 is then displayed. The left side of the Viewer screen displays a list of files in the current directory; the right side shows the current worksheet. If you want to see what's in one of the files in the left column, use the arrow keys or the mouse to move the highlight to the file you want to view. The contents of the file are displayed on the right side of the Viewer screen.

39

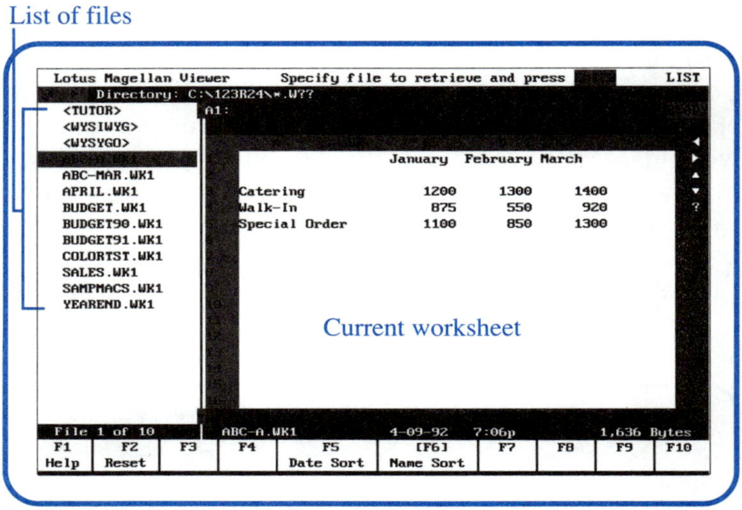

Lesson 8

Figure 8.3 The Viewer screen.

You cannot, however, edit or modify the file in any way. Viewer simply allows you to see what the file contains before you actually retrieve the file. To retrieve the file, return to 1-2-3 by pressing Esc twice, and use the /File Retrieve command as usual.

Removing an Add-In

To remove an add-in from memory, follow these steps:

1. From within 1-2-3, press / (slash).

2. Select Add-In.

3. Select Detach.

4. Choose the add-in name and press Enter. Select Quit to return to READY mode.

Lesson 9
Working with Ranges

In this lesson you'll learn to select, work with, and name ranges in your worksheet.

Why Use Ranges?

The term *range* in 1-2-3 refers to a group of contiguous cells. While some operations you perform affect the entire worksheet (such as some global formatting commands), for other operations you need to highlight a range. You'll use ranges, for example, when you want to perform the following tasks:

- Copy a column or row of numbers to another part of the worksheet.
- Total a column or row of numbers.
- Delete a section of the worksheet.
- Change the format for a portion of the worksheet.
- Move a block of cells.

Lesson 9

Range A range is any rectangular block of cells you highlight to perform certain operations.

For many operations in which you'll be specifying ranges—such as copying or moving a block of cells—1-2-3 prompts you to enter a range. In other cases, such as when you are entering a range in a formula, you must decide when to enter a range.

Selecting a Range

In 1-2-3, a range can be as small as one cell or as large as the entire worksheet. You can select a range four different ways:

- Type the cell addresses for the range.

- Use the cell pointer or directional arrows to point to the range.

- Click and drag the mouse to highlight the range.

- Enter a name you've already assigned to the range.

Typing Cell Addresses

First, retrieve the example spreadsheet you've been using so far. Then try the following copy procedure to learn how to type a range when 1-2-3 prompts you to. To start the procedure, follow these steps:

1. Position the cell pointer on cell C3.

2. Display the Main menu by typing / (slash).

Working with Ranges

3. Choose Copy. In the control panel, 1-2-3 asks you to Copy what? (see Figure 9.1).

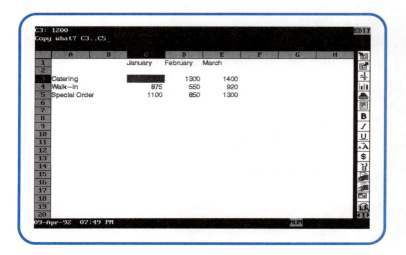

Figure 9.1 The prompt to enter a range for a copy procedure, with a range specified.

4. Type the cell address where you want the range to start (in this case, c3). 1-2-3's default values disappear.

5. Type two periods (..).

6. Type the cell address that marks the place you want the range to end (in this case, c5). The range you specified looks like C3..C5, as shown in Figure 9.1.

7. Press Enter. 1-2-3 continues with the copy procedure and asks you to provide another range indicating where you want to place the copy. For now, back out of the copy procedure by pressing Esc until you return to the worksheet in READY mode.

43

Lesson 9

Pointing to a Range

Try the same basic procedure to illustrate pointing to a range. With the active cell at cell C3, follow these steps to point to the range:

1. Position the cell pointer on cell C3.

2. Display the Main menu by typing / (slash).

3. Choose Copy. In the control panel, 1-2-3 asks you to Copy what? (see Figure 9.1).

4. Use ↓ to highlight cells C3 through C5.

5. Press → until all cells through E5 are highlighted.

6. Press Enter.

When you press Enter, 1-2-3 automatically enters the range you pointed to and continues with the copy procedure, asking you to specify the point on the worksheet where you want to place the copy. For now, press Esc repeatedly to return to READY mode.

If you are using a mouse, you can point to the range by following the steps below.

1. Position the cell pointer on cell C3.

2. Display the Main menu by typing / (slash).

3. Choose Copy. In the control panel, 1-2-3 asks you to Copy what? (see Figure 9.1).

4. Point to cell C3.

———————————————————————— Working with Ranges

5. Press and hold the left mouse button.

6. Drag the mouse until cells C3..E5 are highlighted.

7. Release the mouse button.

Deselecting Ranges To deselect a range, press Esc or move the mouse pointer away from the selected range and click the mouse button.

Naming Ranges

If you use certain ranges repeatedly in your spreadsheet, you may want to assign a name to the range so that you don't have to use the pointing or typing methods each time you need to specify a range. For this reason, 1-2-3 allows you to assign a range name to any range you use often.

To assign a range name to a block of cells, follow these steps:

1. Press / (slash) to display the Main menu.

2. Select Range.

3. Choose Name.

4. Choose Create.

5. When 1-2-3 prompts you to Enter name:, type the range name you want (for the sample worksheet, type JANSALES) and press Enter (see Figure 9.2).

Lesson 9

6. Select the range you want to name by either pointing to or typing the range addresses (for this example, choose cells C3..C5).

7. Press Enter. 1-2-3 assigns the range name to the cell range you specified.

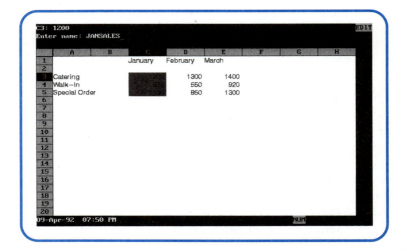

Figure 9.2 Assigning a name to a range of cells.

To see how to use a range name when you're asked to specify a range, try this example:

1. Press / (slash) to display the Main menu.

2. Select Copy.

3. At the Copy What? prompt, type JANSALES.

4. Press Enter. 1-2-3 accepts that range as the range you want to copy from and continues the copy operation, asking you where you want to place the copy. Again, press Esc repeatedly to back out of the copy operation.

Displaying Range Names

1-2-3 lets you display a list of range names so that you can choose the one you need. To display the range names for the current worksheet:

1. Start an operation that prompts you for a range (you can use the copy procedure as an example, if you choose).

2. When 1-2-3 is in POINT mode (shown by the indicator at the top right corner of the screen), press F3 (Names).

   Scroll through the list using the arrow keys until the range name you want is highlighted; then press Enter to select the range.

Deleting Range Names and Erasing Ranges

At first glance, deleting and erasing may look the same. In 1-2-3, they're not.

- When you delete a range, you are deleting the name of the range.

- When you erase a range, you are removing the data in the range.

Deleting a Range Name

1. Display the Main menu by pressing / (slash).

2. Choose the Range command.

Lesson 9

3. Select Name.

4. Select Delete.

5. From the list of displayed range names, highlight the name you want to delete. For example, highlight JANSALES.

6. Press Enter. 1-2-3 then deletes the range name you assigned to that range of cells and returns to READY mode.

Erasing a Range

1. Display the Main menu by pressing / (slash).

2. Choose the Range command.

3. Select Erase.

4. When 1-2-3 asks for the range to be erased, enter the range name, or type or point to the cell range.

5. Press Enter. 1-2-3 erases the contents of the cells in the range you specified.

Lesson 10
Using Formulas and Functions

In this lesson you'll learn to add formulas to your worksheet.

What Is a Formula?

Put simply, a formula is an equation in 1-2-3. A formula can be as simple as 1+1 or as complicated as an equation to figure out a logarithmic value. You'll use formulas in 1-2-3 when you want to perform a vast number of operations, such as:

- Finding the total of a group of numbers.
- Determining the average of a range of cells.
- Performing statistical analyses on groups of numbers.
- Creating a "what-if" analysis based on changing numeric factors.

1-2-3 provides you with a set of special functions that can perform different tasks for you. Many of the formulas you create may include functions, but using a function in a formula is not mandatory.

Lesson 10

Entering a Formula

For this lesson you'll start with a basic formula that doesn't include a function. The next section shows you how to use functions.

Suppose that, using the spreadsheet example set up in earlier lessons, you want to add the values in cells D3 through D5 and place the result in cell D8. To do this, follow these steps:

1. Load the sample worksheet.

2. Use the arrow keys or the mouse to move the cell pointer to cell D8.

3. Press +. 1-2-3 formulas must begin with a number or one of the following symbols: + − @ . (or $. Logical formulas may begin with #.

4. Type D3+D4+D5.

5. Press Enter. 1-2-3 calculates the result and displays it in cell D8 (see Figure 10.1). Line 1 of the control panel displays the formula.

Using Operators in Formulas

Operators tell 1-2-3 how to work with the values in the formula. The operators allowed in 1-2-3 formulas are shown in Table 10.1.

Using Formulas and Functions

Cell D8's formula

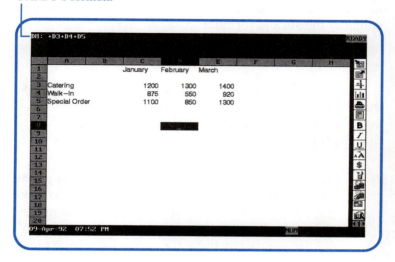

Figure 10.1 Using a formula to total a column.

Table 10.1 Operators used in formulas.

Operator	Description
+	Addition
−	Subtraction
*	Multiplication
/	Division
^	Exponentiation
>	Greater than
<	Less than
>=	Greater than or equal to
<=	Less than or equal to
<>	Not equal to

51

Lesson 10

You also use parentheses to show how you want 1-2-3 to carry out the execution of the formula. For example, consider the simple formula

4-3+2

If you place parentheses around the first two values so that the formula reads (4-3)+2, the result is 3. However, if you place the parentheses around the second two values so that the formula reads 4-(3+2), then the result is −1.

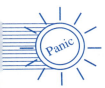

If Your Formula Doesn't Work If you get an error when you try to enter a formula, check to make sure that (1) you have entered a closing parenthesis for each opening parenthesis, and (2) you haven't inadvertently entered a comma in the wrong place.

Using Functions in Formulas

1-2-3 comes with a set of preset functions you can use in your worksheet. (These functions are explained in more detail in a table of functions included at the back of this book.) All functions must begin with an @ sign.

For example, you could total a column of values by using the @SUM function. Try the following example:

1. Load the sample worksheet.

2. Use the arrow keys to move the cell pointer to cell C8.

3. Type @SUM(.

4. Enter the range of cells you want to total by pointing to the range, typing the range reference, or entering a

52

Using Formulas and Functions

range name. (For the example, enter JANSALES, because you named that range in Lesson 8.)

5. Type the closing parenthesis.

6. Press Enter. 1-2-3 places the result in cell C8 (see Figure 10.2). The control panel displays the function.

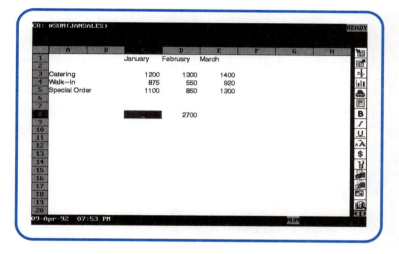

Figure 10.2   The result of using a function in a formula.

Thinking Ahead   At this point, save your sample worksheet (ABC-A.WK1), so you can return to it later. Lesson 6 explains saving procedures.

Lesson 10

Editing a Formula

Inevitably, you'll want to edit formulas and data in your worksheet after you enter them. 1-2-3 makes this easy, as in the following steps:

1. Place the cell pointer on the cell containing the formula you want to edit.

2. Press F2 (Edit).

3. Edit the formula, using the Backspace key to delete incorrect characters.

4. Press Enter. 1-2-3 completes the change, and returns to READY mode.

Displaying Formulas

Although usually you'll want to work with the regular display of 1-2-3, the program gives you the option of displaying all the formulas you've created in their appropriate cells. To show the formulas in the worksheet, follow these steps:

1. Display the Main menu by pressing / (slash).

2. Choose Worksheet.

3. Select Global.

4. Choose Format.

5. Choose Text. 1-2-3 displays all the formulas in the appropriate cells on-screen (see Figure 10.3).

Using Formulas and Functions

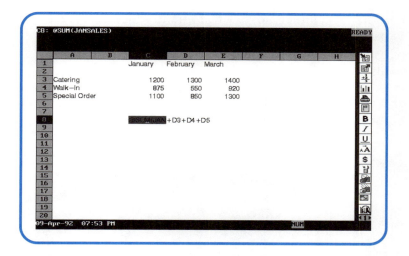

Figure 10.3   Displaying formulas in the worksheet.

Returning to Normal Display   Change the formulas back into values by selecting /Worksheet Global Format General.

Using the Auditor

Lotus 1-2-3 Release 2.4 includes an add-in program, called the Auditor, that allows you to examine and error-check all the formulas in your spreadsheet.

The Auditor can help you:

- Determine which cells depend on a particular formula.
- Find all formulas on the worksheet.
- Locate any circular references.
- Show all formulas in order of calculation precedence.

Lesson 10

The Auditor is an add-in program, which means you use it while you are working with 1-2-3. Because the Auditor uses memory, you won't want to keep the Auditor loaded at all times.

When you invoke the Auditor, 1-2-3 displays the Auditor Settings dialog box (see Figure 10.4).

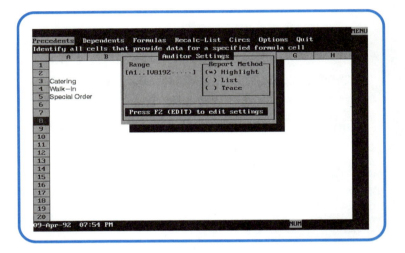

Figure 10.4 The Auditor Settings dialog box.

To edit the options, press F2. Press M. Choose one of the following report methods and press Enter, or click on the option name and select OK:

- Highlight, which highlights the cells found.

- List, which lists the cells.

- Trace, which lets you examine each cell individually.

Press R and type the range containing the formulas you want to examine. Then press Enter twice.

56

Using Formulas and Functions

Use the arrow keys to select the Auditor operation. Press Enter. Type a source cell, if Auditor asks for one. Press Enter. Auditor performs the operation you requested. Table 10.2 lists the options and brief descriptions of each.

Table 10.2 Auditor operations.

Option	Description
Precedents	Finds all cells referred to in formulas in a specified range.
Dependents	Finds dependent cells to the formulas in a range.
Formulas	Locates all formulas in a range.
Recalc-List	Identifies formulas in their order of calculation.
Circs	Finds all circular references.
Options	Sets options for range or mode of audit.
Quit	Returns you to 1-2-3.

When you are ready to detach the Auditor from memory, follow these steps:

1. Press / (slash).

2. Select Add-In.

3. Choose Detach.

4. Select AUDITOR from the list and press Enter. Then select Quit to return to READY mode.

In this lesson you learned how to enter, edit, and display formulas. You also learned how to use the Auditor to examine and error-check formulas in your worksheet. In the next lesson, you will learn how to copy and move cells.

Lesson 11
Copying and Moving Cells

In this lesson you'll learn various methods for copying and moving cells.

Understanding Relative and Absolute Cell Referencing

In Lesson 2 you learned how to read a cell's address. There's another aspect to cell addressing that you need to know before you copy or move cells in your worksheet. 1-2-3 gives you the option of assigning cells absolute or relative addresses when you *reference* (specify) the cells in a formula.

By default, all cell references in formulas are *relative*. If you move or copy a formula with relative cell addresses, the formula's cell addresses change to reflect the formula's new place in the worksheet. When you assign a cell an *absolute* address in a formula, the address of the cell will not change when you move or copy the formula.

Consider this example. The formula +C3*(C5-D5) in cell D6, contains relative addresses. The contents of D5 are subtracted from C5, and then the result is multiplied by the contents of C3. If C3 = 5, C5 = 8, and D5 = 2, the result is 30.

If you copy the formula to another location, the cell references (and, therefore, the contents of the cells) change. Suppose that you copy the formula to M20, which is 14 cells down and nine cells right of D6. The formula now reads L17*(L19-M19). Each cell address in the copied formula is 14 cells down and 9 cells right of the corresponding address in the original formula. You simply copied the formula, but 1-2-3 automatically adjusted the cell addresses so that the correct values would be used in the formula: L17 = 4, L19 = 6, and M19 = 4. The result is 8.

When you assign absolute addresses in a formula, the cell references do not change. Therefore, the formula would remain the same no matter where on the worksheet you placed the copied formula. (If the formula contains some relative and some absolute references, only the relative references change to reflect the new location.)

To assign an absolute address to a cell, enter a dollar sign ($) before both the column and row of the cell address, such as +C3*(C5-D5).

To create an absolute address for a cell, you can:

- Type the dollar signs in the appropriate places as you enter the formula.

- Press F4 (Abs) twice at the place in the formula you want 1-2-3 to add the dollar signs for you. For example, type D5 and press F4 twice. The cell address appears as D5. If you continue to press F4, various combinations of relative and absolute values will appear, from which you can choose.

Before you copy or move cells, be sure to examine the formulas in your worksheet to see whether you need to assign any absolute addresses.

Lesson 11

Mixed Addressing 1-2-3 also allows you to create a mixed address, which mixes absolute and relative addressing. See *The First Book of Lotus 1-2-3 Release 2.4*, from Sams, for more information.

Copying Cells

With 1-2-3, you use the Copy command to copy a cell or a range of cells. You have four options for the type of copy operation you can perform:

- You can make a copy of one cell.

- You can copy one cell into many cells.

- You can make a copy of a range of cells.

- You can copy one range to a larger range of cells.

To copy cells, follow these steps:

1. Return to the sample worksheet.

2. Display the Main menu by pressing / (slash).

3. Select Copy (see Figure 11.1).

4. The Copy what? prompt appears. If you are copying a single cell, position the cell pointer on that cell or type the cell address. If you are copying a range of cells, point to or type in the range of cells you want to copy. (For this example, type C3..C5 after the prompt.)

60

Copying and Moving Cells

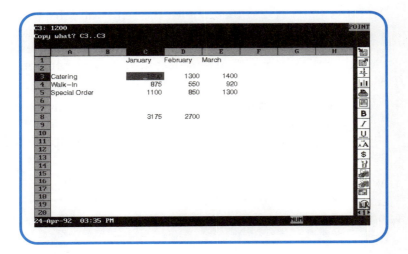

Figure 11.1 Choosing the Copy command.

5. Press Enter.

6. The To where? prompt appears.

   • If you are copying a single cell to another single cell, place the pointer on that cell, or type the address.

   • If you are copying a range of cells to a range of the same size, position the cell pointer at the beginning cell of the range where you want to place the copy, or type that cell's address. (For this example, move the pointer to F10.)

   • If you are copying a single cell or a range of cells and placing the copy into a larger range—for example, suppose you want to copy C3..C5 to a larger block of the worksheet such as F10..H20—either type the range of cells you want to receive the copy, or highlight the range you want to copy to.

61

Lesson 11

7. Press Enter. 1-2-3 then copies the range of cells you specified (see Figure 11.2). Any formulas included in that range are also copied and their cell references automatically modified to reflect their new placement.

The Copy SmartIcon allows you to copy a selected range quickly. Select the range to be copied from, choose this SmartIcon from palette 3, and then choose the destination range.

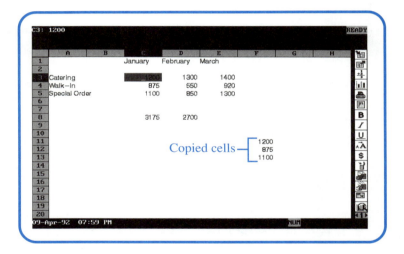

Figure 11.2 The completed copy procedure.

Moving Cells

The move procedure is similar to the copy procedure. Instead of placing a duplicate of a cell or a range of cells at another point in the worksheet, however, 1-2-3 moves the cells to another location.

Copying and Moving Cells

To move cells, follow these steps:

1. Display the Main menu by pressing / (slash).

2. Choose Move.

3. At the Move what? prompt, point to or type the address of the cell or range of cells you want to move. For this example, type D3..D5.

4. Press Enter.

5. At the To where? prompt, point to or type the cell address of the cell in the upper left corner of the range where you want to place the moved cells. (For this example, position the cell pointer on cell D10.)

6. Press Enter. 1-2-3 then removes the cells from their position in the worksheet and places them at the new location.

Another way to move a selected range is with the Move SmartIcon on palette 5. Remember that you must select the range to be moved before selecting this SmartIcon.

Returning to the Old Worksheet   Return to the last saved version of the worksheet by using /File Retrieve and choosing the same file again.

In this lesson you learned about relative and absolute cell addressing and found out how to copy and move cells. In the next lesson you'll learn how to edit the contents of cells and delete cells you no longer need.

Lesson 12
Editing and Deleting Cells

In this lesson you'll learn how to edit cell contents and delete unneeded cells. You'll also learn about manual and automatic recalculation.

Editing Cells

Editing is easy with 1-2-3. Place the cell pointer on the cell you want to modify and then press F2 to change 1-2-3 to EDIT mode. The contents of the cell appear in the display panel. You then can use a variety of keys to edit the contents of the cell as necessary (see Table 12.1).

Table 12.1 Editing keys in EDIT mode.

Key	Action
Esc	Removes all characters in edit line.
Del	Deletes character at cursor position.
Backspace	Removes character to the left of the cursor.
Ins	Changes between INSERT and OVERTYPE modes.
→	Moves cursor one character to the right in edit line.
←	Moves cursor one character to the left in edit line.

Editing and Deleting Cells

Key	Action
Tab	Moves cursor five characters right.
Shift-Tab	Moves cursor five characters left.
Ctrl-→	Moves cursor five characters right.
Ctrl-←	Moves cursor five characters left.
Home	Moves cursor to beginning of edit line.
End	Moves cursor to end of edit line.

To edit a cell, follow the steps below. If you are following the example, retrieve the example worksheet (with the /File Retrieve command) before you begin.

1. Position the cell pointer on the cell you want to edit.

2. Press F2 (Edit). 1-2-3 displays the EDIT indicator in the upper right corner (see Figure 12.1).

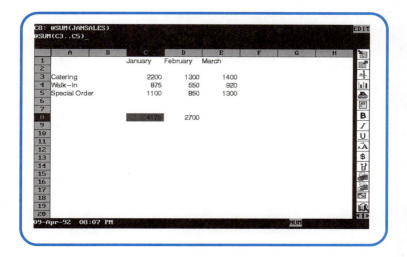

Figure 12.1 Editing worksheet cells.

65

Lesson 12

3. Edit the cell as necessary (using the keys in Table 12.1).

4. Press Enter. 1-2-3 then records your changes and returns the worksheet to READY mode.

No Forwarding Address... When you edit cell formulas, remember whether the cell addresses should be relative or absolute. If you edit a formula that contains absolute addresses and forget to reassign the absolute cells (see Lesson 10), you may wind up with unexpected—and erroneous—results.

Setting Recalculation

Anytime you edit information on your worksheet, you will undoubtedly find formulas that need to be recalculated. You can have 1-2-3 automatically recalculate your worksheet for you after any change or addition (this is known as *automatic recalculation*), or you can have the program recalculate the spreadsheet only when you specify (known as *manual recalculation*). The 1-2-3 default is automatic recalculation.

To change to manual recalculation, follow these steps:

1. Display the Main menu by pressing / (slash).

2. Choose Worksheet.

3. Select Global.

4. Select Recalculation.

5. Choose Manual (see Figure 12.2).

Editing and Deleting Cells

6. Press Enter.

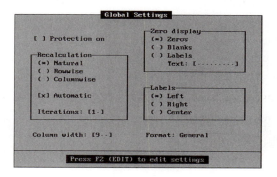

Figure 12.2 Choosing manual recalculation.

When you return to the worksheet, 1-2-3 will recalculate the spreadsheet only when you press F9 (Calc). If, at a later time, you want to change back to automatic recalculation, repeat steps 1 through 4 and then choose Automatic instead of Manual.

 The Calc SmartIcon, from icon palette 3, acts exactly like the F9 (Calc) key in recalculating formulas.

Deleting Cells

To erase the contents of a single cell, follow these steps:

1. Position the cell pointer on the cell you want to erase.

2. Press / (slash) to display the Main menu.

3. Select Range.

4. Select Erase (see Figure 12.3).

67

Lesson 12

5. Press Enter. 1-2-3 then removes the contents of the cell and displays the blank cell in the worksheet.

Use the Delete SmartIcon to erase cells. Highlight the range to be erased, then select this SmartIcon from palette 4.

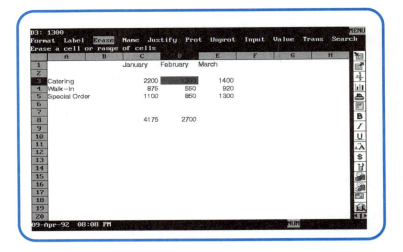

Figure 12.3 Choosing /Range Erase.

Deleting Rows and Columns You may want to delete an entire row or column on your worksheet. This technique is explained in Lesson 16.

In this lesson you learned to edit and delete cells in the worksheet. You also learned how to recalculate formulas. In the next lesson you'll learn how to format the values and labels in your spreadsheet.

Lesson 13
Formatting the Worksheet

In this lesson you'll learn to change the numeric format for portions of the worksheet and for the entire worksheet.

1-2-3 gives you more than one option for formatting the data in your spreadsheet. You can change the format of selected cells (known as *formatting a range*), or you can change the format of the entire worksheet (known as *global formatting*).

Formatting Ranges

You use the /Range Format command to change the format for a range of cells. Select this command to display the format options in the control panel. Table 13.1 explains each of the options available.

Figure 13.1 shows the addition of another column, Averages, in the sample worksheet. This column includes decimal values. For this example, use the Fixed format to suppress the decimal display and round the fractional values. Take a minute to enter the values shown in Figure 13.1.

Lesson 13

Adding Averages To add the Averages column to your worksheet, first enter the column heading by typing it into cell G1. Then use the @AVG function to calculate the values. Enter @AVG(followed by the range you want to average (in this case, C3..E3, C4..E4, and C5..E5). Don't forget to enter the final parenthesis to close the @AVG function.

Table 13.1 Numeric formats.

Format	You Enter	1-2-3 Displays
Fixed	23.89	24
Scientific	–32	–3.20E+01
Currency	1423789	$1,423,789
(Comma)	987654	987,654
General	23.23	23.23
+/–	5	+++++
Percent	.075	7.5%
Text	+C3+C4+C5	+C3+C4+C5
Hidden	123	

Then follow these steps:

1. Position the cell pointer on cell G3 of the example worksheet.

2. Press / (slash).

3. Select Range.

4. Select Format.

5. Select Fixed.

6. Type 0 at the prompt for the number of decimal places.

7. Press Enter.

8. When prompted to enter the range you want to format, press ↓ twice, highlighting G3..G5.

9. Press Enter. 1-2-3 suppresses the display of decimals and rounds the numbers to the nearest integer (see Figure 13.2).

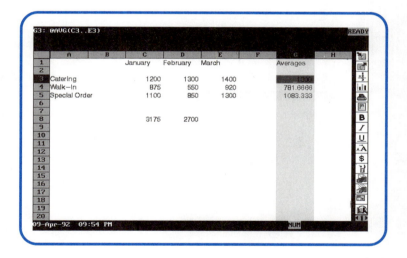

Figure 13.1 The worksheet with an added column in Fixed format.

These SmartIcons can be used to format ranges quickly. The Currency SmartIcon applies the default Currency format with two decimal places. The Percent SmartIcon applies the Percent format with two decimal places. The Fixed SmartIcon

Lesson 13

applies the Fixed format using the default thousands separator. To format quickly, select the range you wish to format, and then select one of these icons from palette 2. Select the icon again to remove formatting applied with it.

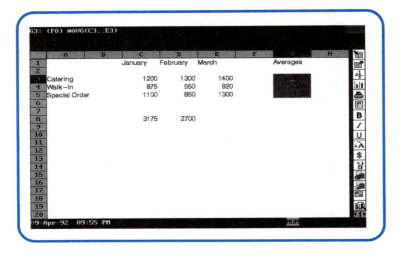

Figure 13.2 The worksheet after range G3..G5 is formatted to round the numbers.

Formatting the Entire Worksheet

1-2-3 gives you the option of changing the format of all values in the worksheet. To do this, use the /Worksheet Global Format command. When you choose this command, you see a list of options identical to those displayed when you used /Range Format.

Formatting the Worksheet

To display all values on the worksheet in Currency format (showing two decimal places):

1. Load the sample worksheet, and then press / (slash).

2. Choose Worksheet.

3. Select Global. (This option tells 1-2-3 you want to change all values on the spreadsheet.)

4. Choose Format.

5. Choose Currency.

6. When 1-2-3 asks how many decimal places you want displayed (2 is the default), press Enter.

I See Stars! Sometimes 1-2-3 will display asterisks instead of numeric values in a worksheet after cells have been formatted. This happens because 1-2-3 doesn't have enough room to display the value in its new format. Widen the column (as described in Lesson 14) to display the value.

Keeping Range Formats Intact When you use /Range Format to change the format of a range, 1-2-3 keeps that setting even when you change the global format of the worksheet.

In this lesson you learned to format values in the worksheet. In the next lesson you'll learn how to change column width.

Lesson 14

Formatting: Changing Column Width

In this lesson you'll learn how to change the width of columns in your worksheet.

1-2-3 automatically displays worksheet columns nine characters wide. If you enter a label that is longer than nine characters, 1-2-3 displays the label anyway; the label appears to cross over into the adjacent cell (if it's empty). If the adjacent cell is not empty, only the portion of the label that will fit in the original cell is displayed. When you enter values that are too large for the spreadsheet, however, 1-2-3 displays asterisks in place of the number as a sign to you that you need to widen the columns in the worksheet.

1-2-3 gives you the choice of widening selected columns (using /Worksheet Column Set-Width) or widening all columns on the worksheet (using /Worksheet Global Column-Width). These options are similar to the other formatting options.

Narrowing Column Width You can also make columns more narrow; the procedure is exactly the same as for widening.

Changing Individual Column Width

Use the following steps to change the width of one column:

1. Position the cursor in the column whose width you want to change. (Choose column C in the sample worksheet.)

2. Press / (slash).

3. Choose Worksheet.

4. Select Column.

5. Select Set-Width.

6. 1-2-3 then prompts you to enter a column width from 1 to 240 characters. (For this example, type 15.)

7. Press Enter. 1-2-3 changes the width of the column, and the numbers display correctly (see Figure 14.1).

Varying Column Width To get the most out of the space you have on-screen, tailor the width of each column to the size necessary for that column. Use /Worksheet Column Set-Width to change the width of each column.

Lesson 14

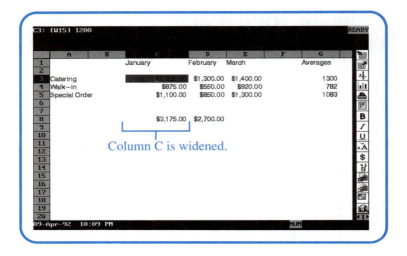

Figure 14.1 Changing the width of one column.

Changing the Width of All Columns

Occasionally, you may want to change the width of all columns on the worksheet. To do this, follow these steps:

1. Open the worksheet.

2. Press / (slash).

3. Choose Worksheet.

4. Select Global.

5. Select Column-Width.

Formatting: Changing Column Width

6. When the `Enter Global Column Width:` prompt is displayed, type a new column width (`10`, for our example).

7. Press Enter.

1-2-3 then changes the width of all columns on the worksheet (see Figure 14.2).

Now all the numbers in the worksheet display correctly, but the new width pushes the Averages column off the screen. Even though you've used the Global command, 1-2-3 leaves the width of column C set at 15.

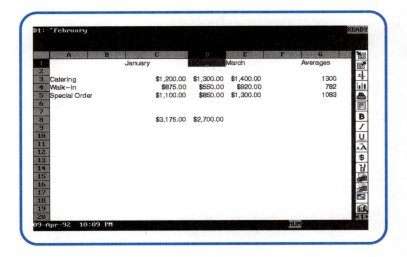

Figure 14.2 All columns are widened to 10 characters, except for C, which was previously set at 15 characters.

Lesson 14

Resetting Column Width

After you've modified the columns on the worksheet, you may decide you liked it better the way it was. You can reset the column width to the default width setting by using the /Worksheet Column Reset-Width command. Try the following example:

1. Press /(slash).

2. Choose Worksheet.

3. Select Column.

4. Select Reset-Width. 1-2-3 then returns the column you specified to the default width.

Changing the Width of a Range of Columns
You can change the width of several columns at one time by selecting the /Worksheet Column Column-Range command.

Hiding Columns

In some cases you may be working with sensitive data. 1-2-3 gives you the option of hiding columns in the worksheet so that you control who sees what. To hide a column in the worksheet, follow these steps:

1. Position the cell pointer on the column you want to hide (in this case, in cell C3).

2. Press /(slash).

Formatting: Changing Column Width

3. Choose Worksheet.

4. Select Column.

5. Select Hide. 1-2-3 displays C3 as the default.

6. Press Enter. 1-2-3 then hides the display of the column (see Figure 14.3). All equations and values in that column are still included in computations performed by the program, so the data is not affected.

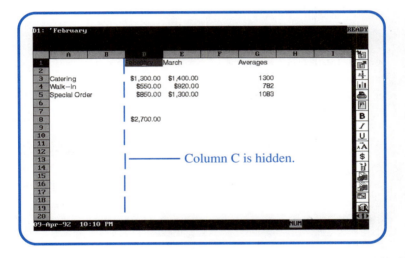

Figure 14.3 Hiding a column.

Printing Peril If you find that all the columns in your worksheet are not printing, check to see whether you have hidden any columns on the worksheet. Hidden columns do not print.

Lesson 14

Redisplaying Columns

To redisplay columns you have hidden on the worksheet, follow these steps:

1. Press / (slash).

2. Choose Worksheet.

3. Select Column.

4. Select Display.

5. When 1-2-3 prompts you to enter the column you want to display, type C3.

6. Press Enter. 1-2-3 then redisplays the column on the worksheet screen.

In this lesson you learned to change the width of columns individually and globally. You also learned how to hide columns and to redisplay hidden columns. In the next lesson you will learn how to align labels in your worksheet.

Lesson 15
Formatting: Aligning Labels

In this lesson you'll learn to align text labels in your worksheet.

Understanding Label Alignment

In earlier lessons you entered column and row labels on your worksheet. When you typed the labels, 1-2-3 automatically aligned the labels along the left edge of the cell (this is known as *left-justification*).

You can tell 1-2-3 how you want the labels to be formatted by entering a label prefix before the label. Table 15.1 lists the label prefixes.

You can change individual labels or change all labels on the worksheet (global) with the alignment options, which are similar to the other formatting commands.

Table 15.1 Label prefixes.

Prefix	Description
'	Aligns the label with the left edge of the cell.
"	Aligns the label with the right edge of the cell.

continues

81

Lesson 15

Table 15.1 Continued.

Prefix	Description
^	Centers the label.
\	Repeats the character you specify.

Changing Alignment of Individual Labels

When you want to change individual labels or a range of cells containing labels, use the /Range Label command. Try the following example:

1. Open a worksheet (for this example, use ABC-A.WK1).

2. Press / (slash).

3. Choose Range.

4. Select Label.

5. Choose the alignment option you want—Left, Right, or Center. (For the sample worksheet, choose Center.)

6. When 1-2-3 asks, type the range of cells you want to align (C1..G1 for this example).

7. Press Enter. 1-2-3 then centers the labels in cells C1..G1 (see Figure 15.1).

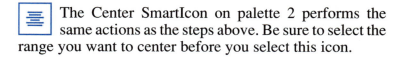 The Center SmartIcon on palette 2 performs the same actions as the steps above. Be sure to select the range you want to center before you select this icon.

Formatting: Aligning Labels

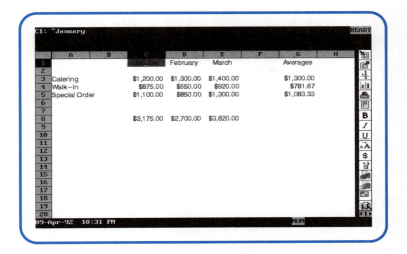

Figure 15.1 Centering labels.

Changing the Default Alignment

1-2-3 allows you to change the default alignment for labels you enter. Change the default alignment—which affects only those labels you enter after changing the default—by using the /Worksheet Global Label-Prefix command.

To change the alignment globally, follow these steps:

1. Press / (slash).

2. Select Worksheet.

3. Select Global.

4. Select Label-Prefix.

5. Choose the alignment option you want—Left, Right, or Center. (For this example, choose Right.)

83

Lesson 15

6. Press Enter. Now each time you enter a new label, 1-2-3 automatically right-justifies the text.

Try the following example to right-justify text:

1. Move the cell pointer to A7 on the sample worksheet.

2. Type TOTALS.

3. Press ←. 1-2-3 enters the label for you, placing it along the right edge of the cell (see Figure 15.2).

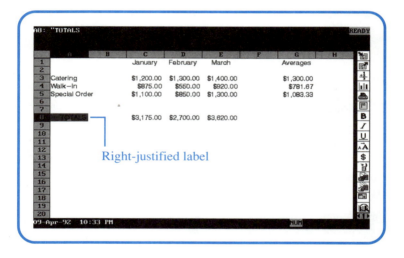

Figure 15.2   Right-justifying labels.

Repeating Labels

You can have 1-2-3 automatically create a label for you by entering a backslash (\) as a label prefix. For example, suppose that you want to add a double-dashed line just above the TOTALS line. To do this, you could use equal

Formatting: Aligning Labels

signs (=) to create the line in the worksheet. Rather than pressing the equal sign several times, you can have 1-2-3 create the label for you.

To create a repeating label, follow these steps:

1. Position the cell pointer where you want to enter the repeating label (in A6 for this example).

2. Type \=.

3. Press Enter. 1-2-3 fills the cell with = characters, creating the label for you. You can then use the /Copy command to copy the characters across the worksheet (see Figure 15.3).

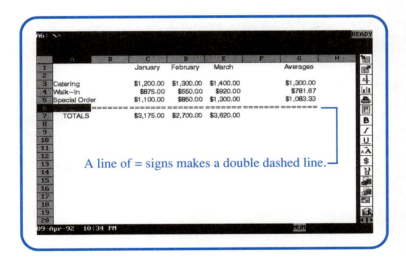

Figure 15.3   Using the \ label prefix.

In this lesson you learned how to align labels in your worksheet. In the next lesson you'll learn how to add and delete rows and columns. This will complete your formatting lessons.

Lesson 16
Working with Rows and Columns

In this lesson you'll learn how to add and remove rows and columns.

Occasionally, you'll need to add a row or column in your worksheet to store data you didn't account for when you began the original worksheet. Adding a blank row or column can help organize your worksheet and make it easier for the reader to understand.

Adding Rows and Columns

To add a row or a column in the worksheet, use the /Worksheet Insert Row or /Worksheet Insert Column commands. Try the following example to add a row to the worksheet:

1. Position the cell pointer in the cell above which you want to insert the row (in the example worksheet, position the cell pointer in A7).

2. Press / (slash).

3. Select Worksheet.

4. Select Insert.

Working with Rows and Columns

5. Select Row.

6. When 1-2-3 prompts you to enter a range, press Enter.

1-2-3 inserts the row at the place you specified and modifies the cell addresses used in any formulas that are affected by the change (see Figure 16.1).

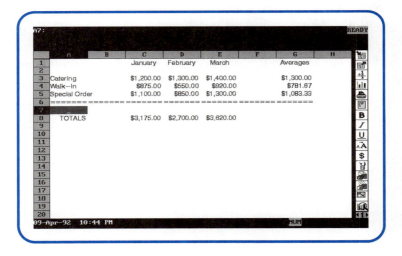

Figure 16.1 A blank row has been inserted between the double dashed line and the totals.

Inserting Columns You can insert a column in the worksheet by using the /Worksheet Insert Column command.

Use these SmartIcons to insert rows or columns into your worksheet. Highlight the row or column below or to the right of where you want to insert, and select one of these SmartIcons from palette 3. Rows are

87

Lesson 16

inserted above the highlighted row. Columns are inserted to the left of the highlighted column.

Deleting Rows and Columns

You can delete a row or column in the worksheet by using the /Worksheet Delete Row or /Worksheet Delete Column commands. Try the following example to delete the row you just added:

1. Position the cell pointer on the cell in the row you want to delete.

2. Press / (slash).

3. Select Worksheet.

4. Select Delete.

5. Select Row.

6. When 1-2-3 prompts you to enter a range, press Enter. 1-2-3 then deletes the row you specified and modifies any formulas affected by the change.

These SmartIcons, also on icon palette 3, delete all rows or all columns, respectively, in the highlighted range.

In this lesson you learned to work with rows and columns. In the next lesson you'll learn how you can use Wysiwyg to enhance the appearance of your 1-2-3 worksheet.

Lesson 17
Using Wysiwyg

In this lesson you'll learn how to use 1-2-3's Wysiwyg add-in to further enhance your spreadsheet.

What Is Wysiwyg?

Wysiwyg stands for What You See Is What You Get. When you add this program into 1-2-3, what you see on-screen closely resembles the printed output you will produce.

You'll discover numerous features in Wysiwyg that allow you to produce presentation-style printouts. Most importantly, Wysiwyg allows you to see your spreadsheet and graphs on-screen as they will appear in print, complete with fonts, borders, and other enhancements.

Attaching Wysiwyg

If Wysiwyg is not attached automatically when 1-2-3 loads, you will need to attach it.

Lesson 17

To load Wysiwyg, select /Add-in Attach, and then select WYSIWYG.ADN from the list of add-in programs. Press Enter. Then press Esc to return to the Main menu.

Figure 17.1 shows the sample worksheet in normal display. When Wysiwyg is active, the screen display changes. The display font and SmartIcons have changed, column letters and row numbers appear differently (see Figure 17.2), and the values in Column G are now visible.

Wysiwyg menus are activated using the : (colon) key in the same way that 1-2-3's main menus are activated using the / (slash) key. To see the Wysiwyg main menu, press :.

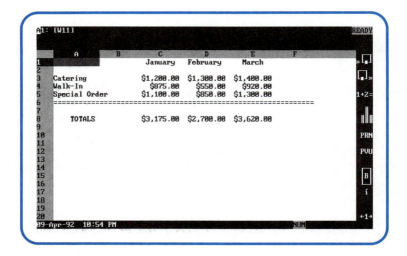

Figure 17.1 Sample worksheet with normal display.

Using Wysiwyg

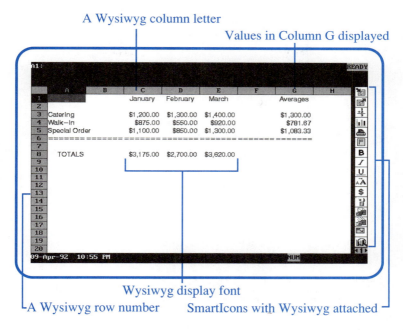

Figure 17.2 The worksheet when Wysiwyg is active.

Changing the Appearance of Text

1-2-3 allows you to change the type you use when you are printing graphs from the 1-2-3 graph printing utility, PrintGraph. You can use Wysiwyg to control the way text appears in your spreadsheets and graph printouts. First, you may need a brief lesson in typography:

> A *typeface*, or *type family*, is a particular design of text. Times and Helvetica are two different typefaces.
>
> A *font* is one size and style of a particular type family. Times 10-point Bold type is an example of one font.

91

Lesson 17

The *type style* is the text enhancement used. In Times 10-point Bold, *boldface* is the type style.

A *point* is a unit of measurement indicating the size of the type. A point is equal to 1/72 of an inch.

The *line height* is the amount of space between lines, measured from the base of one character to the bottom of the character directly below it.

Changing Fonts

To change the font for a particular section of the sample worksheet, follow these steps:

1. Press : (colon) to activate the Wysiwyg menu.

2. Select Format, and then select Font.

3. Press F2.

4. Choose the typeface and size you want by typing the number beside the font or by clicking on that option (in this example, select 2).

5. Press Enter or click OK.

6. When prompted, type the range you want to change (in this case, C1..E1) and press Enter. The worksheet is then displayed with the new font settings in place (see Figure 17.3).

Changing the Default Font Set You can change the default font 1-2-3 uses by selecting :Format Font Default Update and choosing the new default font from the Font Settings dialog box.

Using Wysiwyg

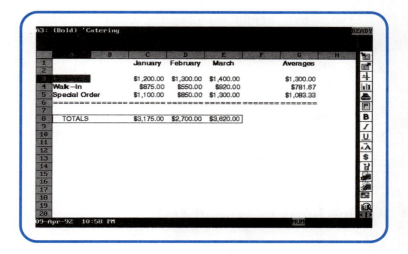

Figure 17.3 The worksheet with a new font, type style, line height, and border.

Changing Line Height

You also can use Wysiwyg to change the amount of space used for each row in the worksheet.

1. Press : (colon).

2. Select Worksheet.

3. Choose Row.

4. Choose Set-Height.

5. Select the row or rows you want to change (in this example, A3..A5).

6. Press Enter.

93

7. Type a new height for the line (the line height is measured in points).

8. Press Enter.

Automatically Setting Line Height You can have Wysiwyg automatically set the line height for you by selecting :Worksheet Row Auto.

Adding Borders Around Text

You can highlight special portions of your spreadsheet by using lines to call attention to particular ranges, columns, or rows. To add a border to a range of worksheet cells, follow these steps:

1. Press : (colon).

2. Select Format.

3. Choose Lines.

4. Choose Outline.

5. When prompted, enter the range (for the example worksheet) and press Enter. Wysiwyg adds a border around the range you specified (refer to Figure 17.3).

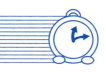
Adding Lines You can also use the :Format Lines command to add lines around individual cells, underneath cells, to the left or right of cells, or above cells. Additionally, you can use a double line to highlight or outline cells.

Selecting a Worksheet Frame

To modify the frame that surrounds your 1-2-3 worksheet, follow these steps:

1. Press : (colon).

2. Select Display.

3. Choose Options.

4. Choose Frame.

5. Choose Special from the displayed options (1-2-3, Enhanced, Relief, Special, or None). Choose Inches. The top of the frame then changes to a ruler line (see Figure 17.4). Choose Quit twice to return to READY mode.

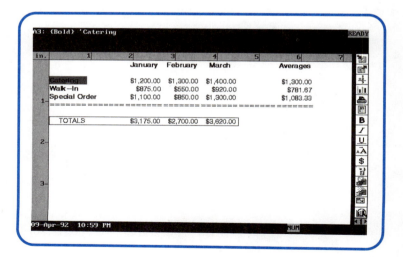

Figure 17.4 The worksheet with the new frame.

Lesson 17

Changing the Worksheet Grid

Wysiwyg also gives you the option of displaying or erasing the grid lines of the worksheet. When you first load Wysiwyg, the grid is turned off. To display the grid, follow these steps:

1. Press : (colon).

2. Select Display.

3. Choose Options.

4. Choose Grid.

5. Choose Yes. Wysiwyg then displays the grid. To suppress the grid, select :Display Options Grid No.

When you no longer need Wysiwyg, you may want to remove it from your computer's memory. Follow the steps in Lesson 7 for detaching an add-in program.

Lesson 18
Printing Worksheets

In this lesson you'll learn how to print the worksheet you've created.

Starting the Print Operation

After you've created, edited, formatted, and enhanced your worksheet, you're ready to print. In 1-2-3, you can print to the printer or a disk file. You can print the entire worksheet, current screenful, or a specified range. In most instances, you'll want to print to the printer to get a hard copy of the work you've done. (You might print to a file, for example, when you are creating a file that will be printed on another computer.)

When you are ready to initiate the print procedure, follow these steps:

1. Press / (slash).

2. Select Print. 1-2-3 displays the Print menu, giving you the option of printing to a file or to the printer (see Figure 18.1).

Lesson 18

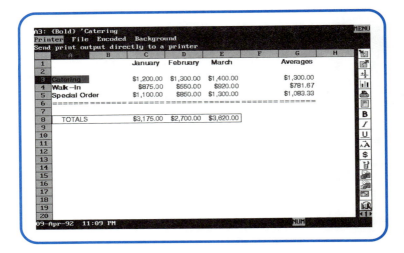

Figure 18.1 The Print menu lets you print to a file or to a printer.

3. Select Printer to send the data to the printer. 1-2-3 displays the subcommands available with the Print menu (see Figure 18.2). Table 18.1 explains each of the commands available in this subcommand list.

4. Select Range.

5. Enter or highlight the range you want to print.

6. If you are using a dot-matrix printer, select Align to tell 1-2-3 that the paper is positioned properly.

7. Select Go. 1-2-3 then prints the worksheet range you specified.

 To print a range, select the range and choose the Print SmartIcon from icon palette 5.

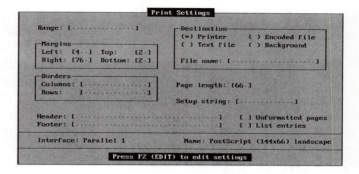

Figure 18.2 The subcommands and Print Settings dialog box available after selecting /Print Printer.

To Stop Printing If you've forgotten something or you've entered the wrong print range, you can stop printing at any time by pressing Ctrl-Break.

Table 18.1 Print menu subcommands.

Command	Use to
Range	Specify the range to be printed.
Line	Move the paper line by line for adjustment.
Page	Advance paper to the top of the next page.
Options	Change the print defaults and enhance printouts.
Clear	Clear any previously entered settings.
Align	Tell 1-2-3 that the current position of the paper is the page top, for dot-matrix printers.
Go	Begin printing.
Quit	Leave the Print menu.

Lesson 18

Inserting Page Breaks You can add a page break within the worksheet by positioning the cell pointer in column A of the row where you want to insert the page break and selecting the /Worksheet Page command. 1-2-3 inserts the page break characters (| ::) at the cell pointer location.

Printing a Screen

You can have 1-2-3 produce a draft-quality printout of only the current screen. You might want to do this, for example, if you are planning to work on a different worksheet and want to have a hard copy of the current worksheet to refer to as you're working on the new worksheet. To print the current screen, follow these steps:

1. Display the portion of the worksheet you want to print.

2. Press Shift-PrtSc.

Adding Headers and Footers

1-2-3 automatically reserves six lines for headers and footers in your worksheet printout: three lines for the header, at the top of the page; and three lines for the footer, at the bottom.

To enter a header or footer for the worksheet printout, follow these steps:

1. Press / (slash).

2. Select Print.

3. Choose Printer.

4. Select Range, and enter the range you want to use for the header.

5. Choose Options.

6. Choose Header or Footer.

7. At the prompt, type the text you want to use in the header or footer, for example

   `ABC Catering, Inc.`

8. Press Enter.

9. After entering the text, choose Quit. 1-2-3 then stores the information with the file and will print the header or footer at print time.

1-2-3 makes things easier for you by giving you a few characters that will substitute dates, page numbers, and alignment information in header and footer lines. Table 18.2 highlights these characters.

Table 18.2 Characters used in headers and footers.

Character	Description
#	Prints the page number at the character position in the header.
@	Prints the system date (DD-MM-YY) in the header or footer.
|	Centers any text following the character.
| |	Right-justifies any text following the second character.

Lesson 18

Printing Worksheet Formulas

Occasionally, you may want a printout of the formulas in your worksheet. This would be particularly important to you, for example, if you have created a series of elaborate formulas that you want to share with others.

To print the formulas from the worksheet, follow these steps:

1. Press / (slash).

2. Select Print.

3. Select Printer.

4. Choose Options.

5. Choose Other.

6. Choose Cell-Formulas to print the formulas.

7. Press Esc.

8. Choose Range.

9. Enter the print range.

10. Select Align to align the page.

11. Select Go to print the range you've specified. 1-2-3 produces a vertical list of cell contents, with the cell address listed first, and then the format, width, and actual cell contents of each cell. Select Quit to return to READY mode.

Lesson 19
Creating a Basic Graph

In this lesson you'll learn to create a simple graph from the data in the 1-2-3 worksheet.

Understanding Graph Types

Graphs help you show trends that you might not see easily from a worksheet full of data. For example, you can use graphs to help illustrate the financial information your worksheet has been number-crunching. Table 19.1 highlights 1-2-3's seven graph types and provides an example of each.

Table 19.1 1-2-3 graph types.

Type	Description
Line	Shows the trend of data over time. For example, you might graph the sales of a particular department over a period of months.
XY	Shows correlations between different types of data. For example, you might compare the company's sales totals with the sales of a particular department. XY graphs are also called scatter graphs.

continues

Table 19.1 Continued.

Type	Description
HLCO	Tracks changes in a single set of data over a fixed period of time. HLCO graphs are used to follow changes in stock prices each day.
Bar	Compares the values in two or more ranges of data. For example, you could use a bar graph to depict the sales of two different products over a period of months.
Stacked-Bar	Shows how individual data items contribute to a total. For example, one bar might represent all of January sales, with segments within that bar showing the sales of individual departments.
Pie	Shows how the values in the series compare to the whole. For example, you might use a pie chart to show annual sales and include a "slice" for each month.
Mixed	Combines a bar graph and a line graph. Mixed graphs are usually used to show two different types of data in a single graph.

The steps involved in creating each type of graph are similar, so there's no need to cover the creation of each type of graph. Instead, this lesson gives examples of how to create the most common graph types: bar and pie. For more information on the other graph types, see *The First Book of Lotus 1-2-3 Release 2.4* (from Sams).

Creating a Bar Graph

For this example, you will produce a bar graph that shows how each of the divisions of ABC Catering did in the first three months of 1992.

When you're ready to create the graph, follow these steps:

1. Press / (slash).

2. Select Graph (see Figure 19.1).

3. Select Type.

4. Choose Bar as the graph type.

5. Select A as the first data range you want to graph.

6. In response to the Enter first data range: prompt, highlight or type the range (C3..E3 for the example worksheet) and press Enter.

7. Select B.

8. Enter the range (C4..E4 for the example).

9. Select C.

10. Enter the range (C5..E5 for the example).

11. Choose X.

12. Enter the range (C1..E1 for the example). This tells 1-2-3 which cells to use as labels along the x-axis of the graph.

13. Select View to display the graph. 1-2-3 displays the graph you have created (see Figure 19.2). Press Esc to return to the worksheet.

Lesson 19

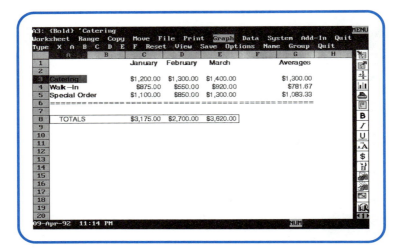

Figure 19.1 The worksheet example, with the Graph command highlighted.

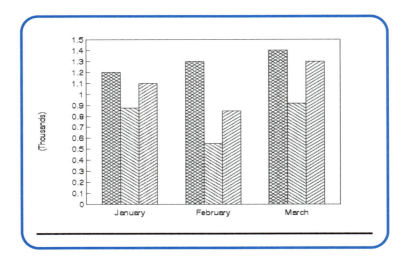

Figure 19.2 The bar graph created from the sample worksheet.

Creating a Basic Graph

 Select the range you want to graph and then select this icon from icon palette 5 to create a quick bar graph.

 No Graph? Depending on the type of display and the amount of memory you have, you may not see a graph when you are using 1-2-3 in Wysiwyg mode. If this happens, return to the Main menu and select Add-In Detach WYSIWYG; then repeat the steps to view your graph.

 Removing Graph Settings If you've previously created a graph, you may have already entered values for the X, A, B, and C data ranges. To remove the settings so that you can enter new ones, select /Graph Reset Ranges.

Creating a Pie Graph

Figure 19.3 shows a sample pie graph. To create it, use the /Graph Type command and choose Pie. You then need only specify an A range (C3..C5) and an X range (A3..A5) because pie charts show only one set of data.

107

Lesson 19

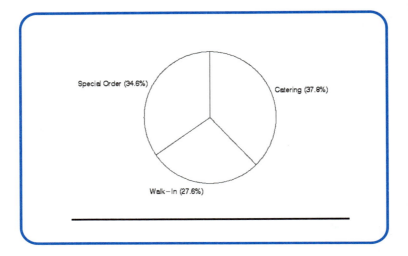

Figure 19.3 A sample pie graph.

In this lesson you learned about the different types of graphs available and created two basic graphs—a bar graph and a pie graph. In the next lesson you'll learn how to enhance the graphs you've created by using /Graph Options.

Lesson 20
Enhancing Graphs

In this lesson you'll learn how to enhance the graphs you've created.

Enhancing the Graph

This lesson shows you how to add titles, a legend, and a background grid to your graph. Additionally, you'll learn to assign a name to a graph and save a graph in a file separate from the worksheet file.

Adding Titles

When you want to add a title to your graph, use the /Graph Options Titles command. Try the following example, using the bar graph created in Lesson 19:

1. Press / (slash).

2. Select Graph.

3. Select Options.

4. Select Titles. 1-2-3 displays yet another subcommand line, giving you the option of selecting titles for the first line, second line, x-axis, or y-axis.

Lesson 20

5. Choose First.

6. After the Enter first line of graph title: prompt, type the first line of your title (ABC Catering for the example graph) and press Enter.

7. Press Enter again when the Titles command is highlighted.

8. Choose Second.

9. Type another line of text (First Quarter Sales for the example graph) and press Enter.

10. Press F10 to view the graph.

1-2-3 adds the first and second line titles you specified (see Figure 20.1). When you're ready to return to the worksheet, press Esc.

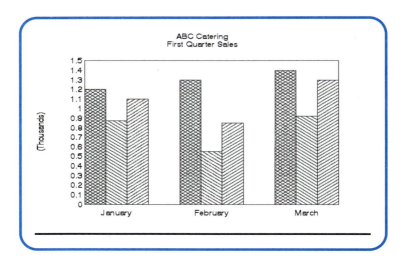

Figure 20.1 Adding titles to the sample bar graph.

Enhancing Graphs

Adding a Legend

You can add a legend to your graphs by using the /Graph Options Legend command. Follow these steps:

1. Press / (slash).

2. Select Graph.

3. Select Options.

4. Select Legend.

5. Select A.

6. At the Enter legend for first data range: prompt, type \ (backslash) and then the address of the cell with the label for the first range of data (A3 in the example) and press Enter.

7. Select Legend and then select B.

8. Type \ (backslash) and the address of the cell with the label for second range (A4 in the example); then press Enter.

9. Repeat steps 7 and 8 to add legends for any other data ranges.

10. Press F10 to view the graph. 1-2-3 then displays the graph complete with titles and legend (see Figure 20.2). Press Esc when you want to return to the worksheet.

All at Once You can enter all the titles, legends, and data labels for your graph in the Graph Legends & Titles dialog box. To see this dialog box, select the /Graph Options command.

111

Lesson 20

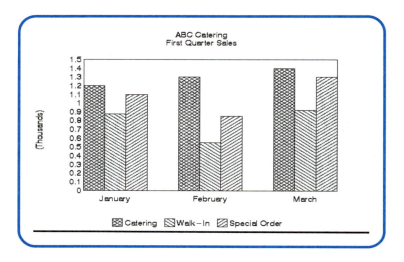

Figure 20.2 The graph with a legend and titles.

Setting a Background Grid

When you first display the graph you create in 1-2-3, the background of the graph is blank. You may, however, want to display a grid so that you can see easily what various data points mean. To set a background grid, follow these steps:

1. Press / (slash).

2. Select Graph.

3. Select Options.

4. Select Grid. 1-2-3 then displays four more options: Horizontal, Vertical, Both, and Clear.

5. Choose an option and press Enter.

Enhancing Graphs

6. Press F10 to view the graph. 1-2-3 adds a grid to the back of your graph (see Figure 20.3).

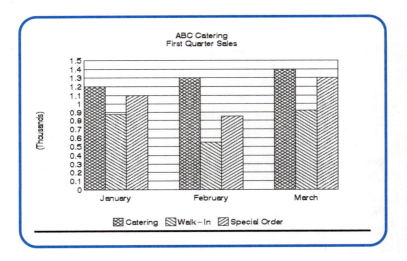

Figure 20.3 Adding a horizontal background grid.

Removing Grid Lines You can remove the grid from the graph by selecting the /Graph Options Grid Clear command.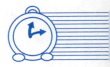

Naming a Graph

In some cases you may want to create more than one graph per worksheet. Using numerous graphs allows you to choose the best representation of the data you have created. Assign a name to a graph by following these steps:

1. Press / (slash).

113

Lesson 20

2. Select Graph.

3. Select Name.

4. Select Create.

5. Type a name for the graph, such as `QTR1SLS`, and press Enter. 1-2-3 then assigns the name to the graph.

Saving a Graph

When you save a worksheet using /Graph Save, 1-2-3 saves the graph with the worksheet and gives the file a .PIC extension. Sometimes, however, you may want to save a graph independent of the worksheet (such as when you want to print the graph from the PrintGraph program). To do this, you use the /Graph Save command, as follows:

1. Press / (slash).

2. Select Graph.

3. Select Save.

4. At the `Enter graph file name:` prompt, type a name for the file.

5. Press Enter. 1-2-3 saves the file, and you can access the PrintGraph program to print the graph if you want.

In this lesson you learned how to enhance the basic graphs you created in the preceding lesson with titles, legends, and grids. You also learned how to save your graph. In the next lesson you'll learn how to use the PrintGraph program to print your graphs.

Lesson 21
Printing a Graph

In this lesson you'll learn to use 1-2-3's PrintGraph program to print the graphs you've created.

Starting PrintGraph

When you are ready to print the graphs you've created, you'll use another part of 1-2-3, known as the PrintGraph program, to print the files. You start the PrintGraph program from within 1-2-3 by following these steps:

1. Press / (slash).

2. Select System.

3. At the DOS prompt, type pgraph.

4. Press Enter. The PrintGraph menu appears (see Figure 21.1).

Memory Problems If you don't have enough memory available to run PrintGraph while 1-2-3 is active, save your worksheet and exit 1-2-3. Then type pgraph at the DOS prompt to start PrintGraph.

115

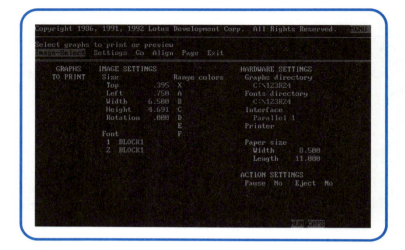

Figure 21.1 The PrintGraph menu.

The PrintGraph Menu

You use the commands in the PrintGraph menu to print the graphs you've created in 1-2-3 and stored as PIC files (see Lesson 20 for information about saving PIC files). Table 21.1 describes the PrintGraph menu commands.

Table 21.1 PrintGraph commands.

Command	Description
Image-Select	Used to select a graph to be printed.
Settings	Controls the graph size, font, color, and orientation.
Go	Begins printing.
Align	Aligns paper in printer.

Printing a Graph

Command	Description
Page	Advances paper one page.
Exit	Exits PrintGraph.

Getting Ready to Print

Use the Settings Hardware command to choose the directories for the graphs and fonts, and to specify the port your printer is connected to and the type of printer you are using. (You chose a printer type when you installed 1-2-3; however, if you installed more than one printer, you can choose which to use at this time.) To specify these options:

1. Start PrintGraph, if you haven't already done so.

2. Choose Settings.

3. Choose Hardware.

4. Choose Graphs-Directory.

5. Backspace over the default, if necessary, and type the directory where your graphs are stored.

6. Press Enter. PrintGraph then inserts the new graph directory.

7. Select Fonts-Directory.

8. Backspace over the default and type the directory where fonts are stored. Then press Enter.

117

9. Choose Printer.

10. When the list of installed printers is displayed, highlight the name of the printer you want to use.

11. Press Enter. PrintGraph then inserts the appropriate printer in the Printer Type: line.

Printing a Simple Graph

When you are ready to print a graph, first make sure your printer is turned on and ready to go. Then follow these steps:

1. Start PrintGraph by using the steps described earlier.

2. Choose Image-Select. PrintGraph searches the directory you specified using the Graph-Directory command and lists the available graphs.

3. Highlight the graph to be printed and press Enter.

4. Select Align.

5. Choose Go. 1-2-3 then prints the graph you selected.

Enhancing the Printout

You can change the size of the graph and way the graph is printed on the page: in portrait mode ($8\frac{1}{2}$" by 11") or in landscape mode (11" by $8\frac{1}{2}$"). You can also change the fonts used and select different colors for the graph.

Changing Size

When you first start PrintGraph, the program will print your graph roughly $6^1/2$" wide and $4^1/2$" tall. The program also gives these options:

- Full, in which the graph is rotated 90 degrees and printed to fill the entire page.

- Half, the default setting, where the graph is printed half the size of an $8^1/2$" by 11" page.

- Manual, in which you can customize the size of the graph by entering your own Width and Height settings.

Controlling Graph Placement Control where the graph prints on the page by setting new Top and Left margins with the Settings Image Size Manual Top (and Left) commands.

To change the size of the graph, follow these steps:

1. Start PrintGraph.

2. Select Settings.

3. Choose Image.

4. Choose Size.

5. Select Full. PrintGraph changes the settings in the IMAGE OPTIONS portion of the screen. The graph will fill the page and print in landscape (11" by $8^1/2$") orientation.

Lesson 21

Adjusting Orientation Change the orientation of the graph by selecting Image Size Manual Rotation and entering 90 for the Rotation setting.

Changing Fonts

You can change the fonts used for graph labels, titles, and legends. To specify a new font, follow these steps:

1. From the PrintGraph menu, select Settings.

2. Choose Image.

3. Choose Font.

4. Select 1 to change the font for the first line of the graph title, or 2 to change the font for all other text in the graph. 1-2-3 displays a list of available fonts.

5. Highlight the font you want to use, press the space bar, and then press Enter to return to the Image menu.

PrintGraph then updates the screen and stores the new settings with the information used at print time.

Lesson 22
Creating a Simple Database

In this lesson you'll learn to build a simple 1-2-3 database.

What Is a Database?

A *database* is any collection of information that you organize in a certain way. For example, a Rolodex represents one database, while a shoe box full of receipts represents another. Anytime you're storing information, you're creating a database.

1-2-3 makes it easy for you to create a database to store a number of important information items, whether you need to record names, addresses, and phone numbers of clients or maintain an elaborate inventory related to your business operations.

Understanding the 1-2-3 Database

The 1-2-3 database doesn't look any different from the worksheet—in fact, you can create the database right in a worksheet file along with your worksheet, or you can create one in its own separate file.

121

If you choose to create the database in the same file as a worksheet, however, be sure to choose a section of the worksheet far away from the worksheet data. This keeps any data-manipulation operations from affecting the numbers on your worksheet.

Table 22.1 lists some database terms you'll see in this and the next lessons.

Table 22.1 Database terms.

Term	Definition
Field	A single information item, such as Address or Phone.
Record	One complete set of fields related to a particular item; for example, if you were creating a client database, one record might consist of Name, Address, City, State, ZIP, and Phone fields.
Database	A file storing a number of records related to a file specific topic; in this example, all client records would be stored in one database file.

Figure 22.1 shows you a simple 1-2-3 database. Within the worksheet structure, one row represents a record, and one cell (the intersection of a column and row) shows an individual field within a record. The entire block of information represents the database itself. The LASTNAME, ADDRESS, CITY, ST, ZIP, and PHONE labels identify the database fields. The row of information about each client, for example, is a record.

Creating a Simple Database

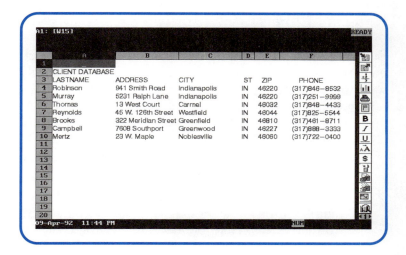

Figure 22.1   A simple database.

Building the Database

There are basically four steps in building a database with 1-2-3: plan the database; enter labels; enter data; and save the database.

The first step in building the database involves planning. For your own databases, think about what type of information you need to include and in what order. You may find writing out the organization of your database helpful before you enter it on-screen.

After you've planned out the database, you're ready to start entering the database labels.

123

Lesson 22

Entering Labels

Before you begin, start a new worksheet or move the cell pointer to a place on your worksheet far away from any worksheet information you have entered. Enter a label by typing the label you want to use and pressing → to move to the next cell. Repeat this step until you've entered labels for all the fields in your database.

Entering Letters and Numbers To enter data that is a mix of letters and numbers (such as stock numbers) or numbers that you want to be able to format as text (like phone numbers) precede the entry with an apostrophe ('). This tells 1-2-3 that entry is a label rather than a value.

Entering Data

Now that you've got the basic organization of the database, you're ready to enter data. Simply position the pointer on the cell in which you want to add information, type the data, and move the pointer to the next cell. Continue until you've entered all the necessary data.

Saving the Database Remember to save your files periodically. Use /File Save to save the file as you would any other spreadsheet file. (For more information about saving files, see Lesson 6.)

In this lesson you learned the basic concepts for building databases using 1-2-3. You also learned how to enter database information and how to save your completed database. In the next lesson you will learn how to sort the records in your database.

Lesson 23
Sorting a Database

In this lesson you'll learn how to sort the data you enter in a database.

Understanding 1-2-3 Sort Operations

Keeping information in a database is pointless unless you have some method for organizing the data. For example, if you have 100 records in a database but no way to alphabetize the clients' names, the only way you can locate a specific record is to scroll through the list until you find the one you want.

1-2-3 gives you several options for sorting the data in the database. By sorting within a certain field (known as a key field), you can organize the data, for example, by LASTNAME, CITY, or ZIP. In fact, you can sort the data based on any of the fields in the database, but some—like PHONE—would be useless in a sort operation.

Key Fields Use *key fields* to specify the sort operation. For example, to sort all the records in your database alphabetically by LASTNAME, the LASTNAME field is the key field.

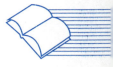

Lesson 23

1-2-3 can sort on one or two key fields. An example of a one-key sort would be alphabetizing all records by LASTNAME. A two-key sort would be first sorting the records by CITY (so that clients from various cities are lumped together and the cities are listed in alphabetical order) and then alphabetizing the records (within the CITY sort) by LASTNAME. In this case, the key fields are CITY and LASTNAME.

Sorting on One Key Field

For this example, you'll alphabetize the client records according to LASTNAME. First, make sure the database portion of the worksheet is displayed on-screen (see the example in Figure 23.1). To sort the records, follow these steps:

1. Press / (slash).

2. Select Data.

3. Select Sort (see Figure 23.2).

4. Select Data-Range.

5. 1-2-3 displays the Enter data range: prompt. Highlight the cells or type the cell addresses of the range you want to sort. Include only the data in the range to be sorted—not the labels. (For the example, type A4..F10.) Press Enter.

6. Select Primary-Key. (This tells 1-2-3 that you are choosing the key field.)

7. Move the cell pointer to any entry in the field you want to use as the key field (for the example database, move the cell pointer to cell A4).

Sorting a Database

8. Press Enter. 1-2-3 displays the Sort Settings dialog box (see Figure 23.3).

9. Type **A** if you want to choose Ascending order or **D** to choose Descending order; press Enter.

10. Select Go. 1-2-3 then sorts the database according to the settings you have chosen.

My Screen Looks Different! To make the example database easier to read, some of the columns and column headings have been realigned. To make your database look like the example, right-align Column F (using the /Range Label command or the Right Alignment SmartIcon) and center the ST, ZIP, and PHONE headings.

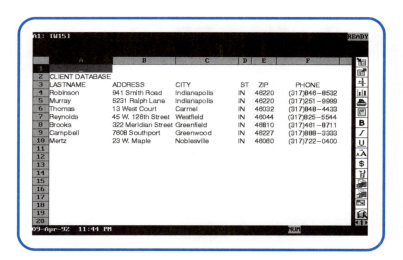

Figure 23.1 The clients' last names are not in alphabetical order.

127

Lesson 23

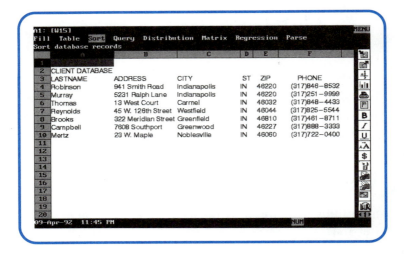

Figure 23.2 The Data menu, with the Sort command highlighted.

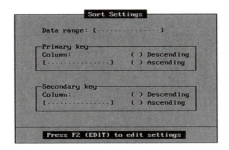

Figure 23.3 The Sort Settings dialog box.

Figure 23.4 shows the records organized alphabetically according to the LASTNAME field.

Sorting a Database

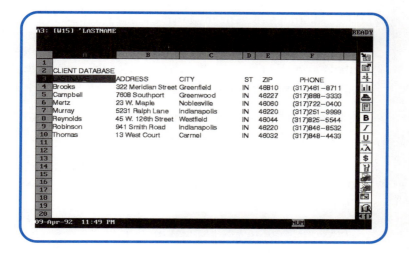

Figure 23.4 The database is sorted by the LASTNAME field.

Sorting on Two Key Fields

As mentioned earlier, 1-2-3 can sort on more than one key field. Try the following example to sort on two key fields:

1. Press / (slash).

2. Select Data.

3. Select Sort.

4. Select Data-Range.

5. 1-2-3 displays the `Enter data range:` prompt. Highlight the cells or type the cell addresses of the range you want to sort. Again, include only the data—not the labels—in the range to be sorted. (For this example, type `A4..F10`.) Press Enter.

6. Select Primary-Key. (This tells 1-2-3 that you are choosing the first key field.)

7. Move the cell pointer to an entry in the field you want to use as the key field (CITY in this example). Press Enter.

8. Choose Ascending or Descending order.

9. Select Secondary-Key. (This tells 1-2-3 that you're selecting the second key field.)

10. Move the cell pointer to an entry in another field (for example, choose A4) and press Enter.

11. Choose Ascending or Descending order.

12. Back at the Sort menu, select Go. 1-2-3 sorts the records.

Figure 23.5 shows the example database sorted first by CITY and then by LASTNAME.

Sorting a Database

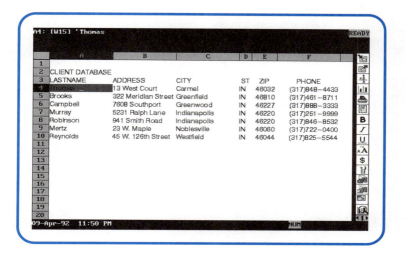

Figure 23.5 The result of the two-key sort.

In this lesson you learned how to sort the records in your database. In the next lesson you learn how to search for specific records in the database.

Lesson 24
Searching for Data

In this lesson you'll learn how to find specific records in the database.

Understanding Search Operations

Searching for specific records is a primary function of any database. Table 24.1 defines some terms you'll need to explore 1-2-3's search feature.

Table 24.1 Terms used in search operations.

Term	Definition
Data query	Requests the database to find a specific record or group of records.
Criteria range	Contains the information on which you base the search.
Output range	Is the cell range where 1-2-3 places the records it extracts or copies from the database.

Searching for Data

Determining the Criteria Range

Suppose, for example, that you want to find all records that have Greenfield entered in the CITY field of a database. The first step is to set up a criteria range so that 1-2-3 knows what information to look for. To create the criteria range, follow these steps:

1. Move to a place on the worksheet away from the database and the worksheet (for this example, use A25).

2. Type CRITERIA RANGE and press ↓.

3. Type the name of the field you want to search (for example, type CITY).

4. Press ↓ again.

5. Type the information you want to search for (for this example, type Greenfield) and press ↓. Your criteria range should look like the one in Figure 24.1.

6. Next, select /Data Query. The Query Settings dialog box shown in Figure 24.2 is displayed.

7. Press F2.

8. Type I.

9. In the Input range: line, type the cell addresses of the database or point to the records you want to include in the search. (For this example, type A4..F10.)

10. Press Tab to move to the Criteria range: line.

11. Type the range containing the criteria field name and data (A26..A27 in the example).

Lesson 24

12. Press Enter twice.

13. Choose /Data Query Find. 1-2-3 then locates the first record that matches the information you specified in the criteria range (see Figure 24.3).

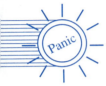

My Screen Looks Different! To make the example database easier to read, some of the columns and column headings have been realigned. To make your database look like the example, right-align Column F (using the /Range Label command or the Right Alignment SmartIcon) and center the ST, ZIP, and PHONE headings.

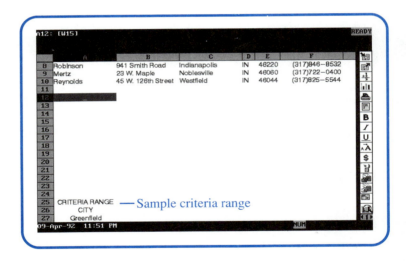

Figure 24.1 The search criteria range.

Searching for Data

Figure 24.2 The Query Settings dialog box.

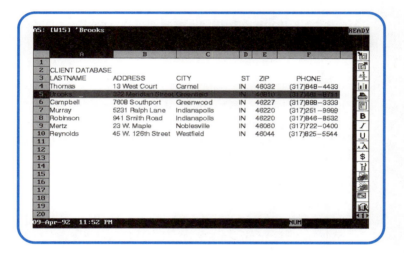

Figure 24.3 Finding the record with the information specified.

Finding Additional Records Press ↓ to move to the next record matching the search information. To end the search, press Esc.

135

Lesson 24

Extracting Records

1-2-3 gives you the option of extracting a group of records—that is, you can copy a group of records from the database and place the copy in another range on the worksheet. To extract a group of records, follow these steps:

1. Select the criteria range.

2. Move to a point on the worksheet below the criteria range (in this case, A30).

3. Type OUTPUT RANGE and press ↓.

4. Copy the field names in the first line of the database and place the copy just below OUTPUT RANGE (cell A31, for example). Your output range would look like the one in Figure 24.4.

5. Select /Data Query Output.

6. When prompted, highlight the row containing the field names in the output range (A31..F31) and press Enter.

7. Select Extract.

8. Press Enter. 1-2-3 copies all records that meet the information in the criteria range and places them in the output range (see Figure 24.5).

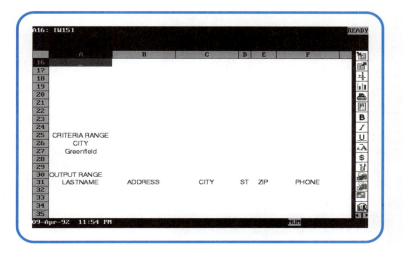

Figure 24.4 Setting up the output range.

Figure 24.5 Performing an extract operation.

Lesson 24

In this lesson you learned some basics of searching for information in the 1-2-3 database. The search process can be somewhat complicated, and, for that reason, you may want to consult *The First Book of Lotus 1-2-3 Release 2.4* to learn more about this subject.

This lesson concludes your course through the *10 Minute Guide to Lotus 1-2-3*. Following this lesson, you will find a Table of Functions, a Table of Features, and a list of the new SmartIcons. These sections are designed to help you learn more about the aspects of the program not covered fully in these lessons. You will also find a DOS Primer covering DOS procedures that you will use with Lotus 1-2-3 Release 2.4.

Overtime

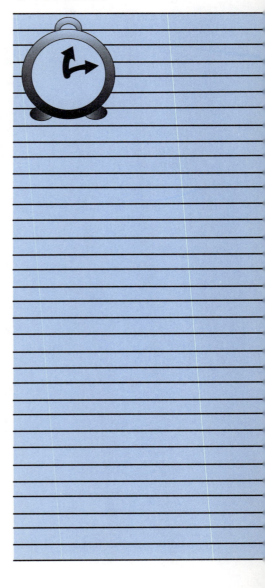

Table of Functions

The following table lists some of the most often-used functions in 1-2-3 Release 2.4. For a complete listing of @functions, see *The First Book of Lotus 1-2-3 Release 2.4*.

Function	Description	Syntax	Example
@ABS	Finds absolute value	@ABS (number)	@ABS (>123.45)
@AVG	Finds average	@AVG (range)	@AVG (C3..C5)
@COUNT	Counts number of cells in a range	@COUNT (range)	@COUNT (A7..N9)
@CTERM	Compounding periods	@CTERM (interest, future, present)	@CTERM (.10/12, 40000, 32000)
@DATE	Calculates the date number	@DATE (year, month, day)	@DATE (92,2,2)
@FV	Finds future value of an investment	@FV (payments, interest, term)	@FV (1100, .075, 24)
@IRR	Finds internal rate of return	@IRR(guess, range)	@IRR(.15, A3..A9)

Function	Description	Syntax	Example
@LN	Finds natural logarithm	@LN (number)	@LN(3)
@LOG	Determines common logarithm	@LOG (number)	@LOG(1000)
@MAX	Finds largest value	@MAX (range)	@MAX (C3..D5)
@MIN	Finds smallest value	@MIN (range)	@MIN (V23..X30)
@NOW	Returns today's date	@NOW	@NOW
@PI	Returns Pi	@PI	@PI
@RAND	Returns a random number	@RAND	@RAND
@RATE	Finds interest rate	@RATE (future, present, term)	@RATE (23000, 18000,50)
@ROUND	Rounds number	@ROUND (number, decimal places)	@ROUND (343.358, 1)
@STD	Finds standard deviation	@STD (range)	@STD (F10..K10)
@SUM	Totals values	@SUM (range)	@SUM (A3..A10)
@TIME	Calculates based on time	@TIME (hour, minutes, seconds)	@TIME (23,9,0)

Table of Features

Feature	Description	To Start
Auditor	Lets you analyze worksheet formulas.	/Add-In Attach **AUDITOR.ADN**.
BackSolver	Recalculates formulas in a worksheet to end with a specified result.	/Add-In Attach **BSOLVER.ADN**.
Bitstream Font Support	Uses Bitstream fonts in worksheets.	Install during 1-2-3's installation.
Database	Creates databases within 1-2-3's column and row format.	Enter data in spreadsheet; use /Data commands.
Data Table	Substitutes variables in certain formulas with values supplied by you.	Use /Data Table command.
Formula	Calculates data using numbers, text, or formulas.	Enter **+**, **−**, **@**, **(**, **#** or **$**; then specify cell addresses or values.
@Functions	Built-in equations you use in formulas to calculate cell values.	Enter the @function name, **(**, the cell addresses, and a closing **)**.

141

Feature	Description	To Start
Graph	Displays trends in data by producing graphs.	Enter data in the worksheet; then use /Graph commands.
Labels	Text you use to label the data in the worksheet.	Enter the label as you want it to appear.
Landscape Mode Printing	Prints along the length of the paper with any supported printer.	:Print Config Orientation.
Linking	Links data in a second worksheet to data in the current worksheet.	Enter +, the file name in double angle brackets (<< and >>), and then the cell to which you want to link the file.
Macro	Automates 1-2-3 operations by recording repetitive keystrokes.	Create the macro; then run it by pressing Alt-F3.
Macro Library Manager	Add-in feature that allows you to create a library of macros you use often.	/Add-In Attach MACROMGR.ADN.
Range	A block of adjacent cells; used in formulas or 1-2-3 operations (such as /Copy or /Move).	Type or point to the first cell address in the range; type two periods (..); and type or point to the ending address.
SmartIcons	Icons that allow you to perform 1-2-3 commands and run macros quickly.	Click on a SmartIcon with the mouse or press Alt-F7 and use the arrow keys.

Table of Features

Feature	Description	To Start
Undo	Lets you cancel the most recent operation or settings changes.	/Worksheet Global Default Other Undo Enable; then press Alt-F4.
Viewer	Lets you view file contents without retrieving them.	/Add-In Attach **VIEWER.ADN**.
Wysiwyg	Allows you to see the work sheet as it appears in print.	/Add-In Attach **WYSIWYG.ADN**.

SmartIcons

Icon	Name	Function
	Add Icon	Adds an icon to the custom palette.
	Align Text	Centers text across selected cells.
	Ascending Sort	Sorts a database in ascending order.
	Background Color	Displays background of selected cells in the next color.
	Bold	Displays the selected cells in bold type style.
	Calc	Recalculates all formulas in the worksheet.
	Center	Centers data in selected cells.
	Circle	Circles selected cells.
	Clear Formats	Restores the default font and clears all other formatting from the range.
	Copy	Copies the selected cells to the range you specify.
	Copy Data	Copies the data in the selected cell to all other cells in the range.

SmartIcons

Icon	Name	Function
	Copy Format	Copies the format of the selected cell to all other cells in the range.
	Currency	Formats selected cells in currency format with two decimal places.
	Delete Column	Deletes the selected column or columns.
	Delete Row	Deletes the selected row or rows.
	Descending Sort	Sorts a database in descending order.
	Double Underline	Double-underlines selected cells.
	Down Arrow	Moves the cell pointer one cell down in the current column.
	Drop Shadow	Places a drop shadow around selected cells.
	Edit Text	Allows you to enter or edit text in a text range.
	End	Moves the cell pointer to the last cell in the worksheet which contains data.
	End Column	Moves the cell pointer to the last cell in the current column which contains data.
	End Row	Moves the cell pointer to the last cell in the current row which contains data.
	Erase	Erases data from the selected cells.

145

Icon	Name	Function
	Fill	Fills the selected cells with a sequence of values.
	Find and Replace	Performs a search and replace operation.
	Fixed	Formats selected cells in fixed format.
	Foreground Color	Displays data in selected cells in the next color.
	Goto	Moves the cell pointer to the cell or range you specify.
	Graph	Graphs the contents of the selected cells.
	Help	Activates 1-2-3's help system.
	Home	Moves the cell pointer to cell A1.
	Home Column	Moves the cell pointer to the first cell in the current column which contains data.
	Home Row	Moves the cell pointer to the first cell in the current row which contains data.
	Horizontal Page Break	Inserts a page break at the current row.
	Insert Column	Inserts a column to the left of the selected column.
	Insert Date	Inserts the current date into the cell.
	Insert Graph	Pastes the current graph into the worksheet.
	Insert Row	Inserts a row above the selected row.

Icon	Name	Function
	Italic	Displays the selected cells in italic type style.
	Larger Type	Displays data in selected cells in the next larger type size.
	Left Align	Left aligns data in selected cells.
	Left Arrow	Moves the cell pointer one cell to the left.
	Move	Moves the selected cells to the range you specify.
	Move Icon	Moves an icon to another location in the custom palette.
	Outline	Outlines selected cells.
	Percent	Formats selected cells in percent format with two decimal places.
	Print Preview	Displays the selected cells as they would appear when printed.
	Print Range	Prints the selected cells.
	Remove Icon	Removes an icon from the custom palette.
	Retrieve	Retrieves a worksheet file.
	Right Align	Right-aligns data in selected cells.
	Right Arrow	Moves the cell pointer one cell to the right.
	Run	Executes a macro.

Icon	Name	Function
	Save	Saves the current worksheet.
	Shade	Shades selected cells.
	Step	Executes macros one step at a time.
	Sum	Sums values in high-lighted cells, or in the adjacent range.
	Underline	Underlines selected cells.
	Undo	Reverses the last command if the Undo feature is enabled.
	Up Arrow	Moves the cell pointer one cell up in the current column.
	User Icon	Displays descriptions of macros attached to user icons U1 through U12.
	Vertical Page Break	Inserts a page break at the current column.
	View Graph	Displays the current graph.
	Zoom	Enlarges the worksheet display.

DOS Primer

This appendix highlights some of the DOS procedures you will use during your work with this program.

DOS is your computer's Disk Operating System. It functions as a go-between program that lets the various components of your computer system talk with one another. Whenever you type anything using your keyboard, whenever you move your mouse, whenever you print a file, DOS interprets the commands and coordinates the task. The following sections explain how to run DOS on your computer and what you can expect to see.

Starting DOS

DOS is probably already installed on your hard disk. When you turn on your computer, DOS automatically loads, and you can begin using your computer.

Changing Disk Drives

Once DOS is loaded, you should see a *prompt* (also known as the DOS prompt) on-screen that looks something like C:\> or C>. This prompt tells you which disk drive is currently active. Here are some guidelines that help determine a drive's letter:

- The hard disk is usually labeled C. (Most computers have only one hard disk, but it may be treated as several disks: C, D, E, F, and so on.)

- The floppy disk drives, located on the front of your computer, are Drives A and B.

- If you have only one floppy drive, it's usually A. If you have two floppy drives, the top or left drive is usually A, and the bottom or right drive is B.

You can activate a different drive at any time by following this procedure:

1. Make sure there's a formatted disk in the drive you want to activate.

2. Type the letter of the drive followed by a colon. For example, type `a:`.

3. Press Enter. The DOS prompt changes to show that the drive you selected is now active.

Making Backups of the 1-2-3 Program Disks with DISKCOPY

Before you install Lotus 1-2-3 Release 2.4 on your hard disk, you should make *backup copies* of the original program disks. By using backups to install or run the program, you avoid the risk of damaging the original disks.

Obtain disks of the same type as your distribution disks. The type of disk should be marked on the package. Because the DISKCOPY command copies the entire disk, you don't have to format the blank disks before you begin.

1. Change to the drive containing the DOS program files.

2. If the DISKCOPY file is in a separate directory, change to that directory as explained earlier. For example, if the file is in the C:\DOS directory, type `cd\dos` at the C prompt, and press Enter.

3. Type `diskcopy a: a:` or `diskcopy b: b:`, depending on which drive you're using to make the copies.

4. Press Enter. A message appears, telling you to insert the source diskette into the floppy drive.

5. Insert the original Lotus 1-2-3 Release 2.4 disk you want to copy into Drive A and press Enter. DOS copies the disk into RAM. When DOS is done copying the original disk, a message appears telling you to insert the target diskette into the floppy drive.

6. Insert one of the blank disks into the floppy drive, and press Enter. DOS copies the disk from RAM onto the blank disk. You may have to swap disks several times before the copy is complete. When the copying is complete, a message appears, asking if you want to copy another diskette.

7. Remove the disk from the drive, and label it with the same name and number as the original disk.

8. If you need to copy another original disk, press Y and go back to step 5. Continue until you copy all the original disks.

9. When you're done copying disks, type N when asked if you want to copy another disk.

10. Put the original disks back in their box and store them in a safe place.

Formatting Floppy Disks

If you don't have a hard disk, you will have to store your data on floppy disks. (Even if you do have a hard disk, you might want to store data on a floppy disk sometimes anyway.) The first step in preparing a floppy disk to store files is to format the disk.

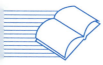

What Is Formatting? *Formatting* creates a map on the disk that tells DOS where to find the information you store on the disk. You cannot place any programs or data of any kind on a new disk before the disk is formatted. *Do not format* your hard disk drive, because formatting erases all programs and information on the hard disk.

1. Start DOS, if it's not already running.

2. Change to the drive and directory that contains your DOS files. For example, if your DOS files are in C:\DOS, type **cd\DOS** at the C prompt and press Enter.

3. Insert the blank floppy disk you want to format in Drive A or B.

4. Type `format a:` or `format b:` and press Enter. The system will tell you to insert the disk (which you've already done).

5. Press Enter. The system then begins formatting the disk. When the format is complete, the system asks whether you want to format another.

6. Press Y if you want to format additional disks, and then repeat all steps. Otherwise, press N to quit.

Labeling Disks   While the disk is being formatted, you can write the labels for the disks. Write on the labels before you attach them to the diskettes. (If you've already placed the labels on the diskettes, write on the labels using a felt-tip pen. The hard point of a pencil or ball-point pen can damage the surface of a diskette.)

Working with Directories

Because hard drives hold much more information than floppy drives, hard drives are usually divided into directories. For example, when you install Lotus 1-2-3, the Installation program suggests that you copy the Lotus 1-2-3 program files to a directory called *123R24* on Drive C. This directory then branches off from the *root directory* of Drive C, keeping all the 1-2-3 program files separate from all the other files on Drive C. Directories can contain subdirectories as well, branching off as branches of a tree would.

Making Directories

To create a directory, you use the MD (Make Directory) command. Follow these steps:

1. Change to the root directory of the drive where you want to create the new directory.

2. At the DOS prompt, type `md\` *directoryname*. (Substitute the name for the directory you are creating in place of *directoryname*, up to 8 characters.)

3. Press Enter. The directory now exists off the root directory. If you want to create a subdirectory off a directory, type the directory name, a backslash and then a subdirectory name, and press Enter.

Another 1-2-3 Directory? You do not need to create a directory to run 1-2-3; the installation program does this for you. You can create additional directories to store your data files, however.

Moving to a Directory

You need to be able to move from directory to directory. To change directories, you use the CD (Change Directory) command:

1. Change to the drive that contains the directory.

2. At the DOS prompt, type `cd\` *directoryname*. (For example, type `cd\123R24`.) The backslash (\) tells DOS to begin at the root directory and move to the directory

you specified under the root. Use the backslash to separate all directories and subdirectories in a command line. For example, to move to a subdirectory of a directory, the command line would look like this:

cd*directoryname**subdirectoryname*

This command line specifies a complete *path* to the subdirectory.

3. Press Enter.

Displaying Directory Contents

To see which files are stored in a directory, use the DIR (Directory) command.

1. Change to the drive and directory whose contents you want to view.

2. Type dir and press Enter. A list of files appears.

If the list is too long to fit on the screen, it scrolls off the top. You can view the entire list by typing /p (pause) or /w (wide) after the DIR command. If you type dir/p, DOS displays one screenful of files; you can see the next screen by pressing Enter. If you type dir/w, DOS displays the list across the screen, fitting many more file names on screen.

Working with Files

DOS also includes commands you can use to work with the files you create. This section briefly introduces the procedures for copying, deleting, and renaming files.

Copying Files

To copy files using DOS, use the COPY command:

1. Move to the directory that stores the file (or files) you want to copy.

2. Type the command line

   `copy filename1.ext drive:\directoryname\filename2.ext`

   In this command line, *filename1.ext* is the name of the existing file you want to copy, *drive:\directoryname* is the drive and directory you want to copy the file to, and *filename2* is the new name you want to give the copy of the file. If you want to create a copy of the file in the same drive or directory, you can omit the path (*drive:\directoryname*) before *filename2.ext*.

3. Press Enter. DOS copies the file and places the copy in the current directory.

Deleting Files

To delete files using DOS, you use the DELETE (or DEL) command:

1. Move to the directory that stores the file you want to delete.

2. Type the command line

   `del filename.ext`

3. Press Enter.

Renaming Files

You use the RENAME (or REN) command to rename files in DOS:

1. Move to the directory that stores the file you want to rename.

2. Type the command line

   `ren filename1.ext filename2.ext`

   In this command line, *filename1.ext* is the name of the existing file, and *filename2.ext* is the new name you want to assign to the file.

3. Press Enter. DOS renames the file and keeps it in the current directory.

For more information about using DOS commands, see *The First Book of MS-DOS* from Sams.

Index

A

absolute cell address, 58-60
/Add-In Invoke command, 38
add-in programs, 36-40
Align command, 99, 116
Alt-F4 (previous worksheet), 35
Alt-F7 (select icon), 20
apostrophe ('), 124
asterisk (*), 73
Auditor add-in program, 55-57
Auditor Settings dialog box, 56
Averages column, 70

B

background grids, 112
backslash (\) key, 12
BackSolver program, 37, 141
Backspace, 64
backups, 150-152
Bad command error message, 2
bar graphs, 104-106
Bitstream Font, 141
borders, 94

C

CALC (Calculator) status
    indicator, 8
CD (Change Directory) command,
    154

cells, 4
    addresses, 5, 42-43, 58-60
    copying, 60-62
    deleting, 67-68
    editing, 64-66
    moving, 62-63
    ranges, 41-42
    referencing, 58-59
check boxes, 17
CIRC (Circle) status indicator, 8
Clear command, 99
clicking, 10
CMD status indicator, 8
columns
    adding, 86-88
    deleting, 88
    hiding, 78-79
    labels, 23-24
    redisplaying, 80
    width, 73-80
command buttons, 17
Control Panel, 3, 6
COPY command, 156
Copy command, 11, 61
Criteria range, 132-134
Ctrl-← (move cursor five
    characters to left), 65
Ctrl-→ (move cursor five
    characters to right), 65
Ctrl-Break (stop printing), 99
cursor, 9
custom palette, 20-21

159

D

data
    entering, 22-26, 124
    locating, 132-134, 137
Data
    menu, 128
    query, 132
    Tables, 141
databases, 141
    creating, 121-124
    entering data, 124
    fields, 122
    labels, 124
    records, 122
    saving, 124
    sorting, 125-130
DEL (Delete) command, 156
dialog boxes, 16
    Auditor Settings, 56
    check boxes, 17
    command buttons, 17
    elements, 17
    Graph Legends & Titles, 111
    items, 17
    list boxes, 17
    option buttons, 17
    Print Settings, 99
    Query Settings, 135
    Sort Settings, 127
    text boxes, 17
DIR (Directory) command, 155
directories, 153-155
Disk Operating System, *see* DOS
DISKCOPY command, 150-151
disks
    drives, 149-150
    floppy, 152-153
    formatting, 152-153
    labeling, 153
DOS, 149-150
dragging, 10

E

EDIT mode, 6, 64-65
editing
    cells, 64-66
    column width, 74-80
    fonts, 92, 120
    formulas, 54
    keys, 64-65
    labels, 82-84
    text, 91-96
    Wysiwyg (What-you-see-is what-you-get), 91-96
End (move cursor to end of edit line), 65
entering
    data, 22-26, 124
    formulas, 50
    labels, 23-24, 124
    values, 25-26
equal sign (=), 84
error messages
    Bad command, 2
    filename, 2
    removing, 8
ERROR mode indicator, 6
Exit command, 117

F

F2 (edit), 54
F3 (display full-screen list), 33
fields, 122
File command, 11
filename error message, 2
files
    copying, 156
    deleting, 156-157
    extension, 15
    naming, 27, 157
    retrieving, 32-33
    saving, 27, 30-31
    see also worksheets

Index

FILES mode indicator, 7
FIND mode indicator, 7
Fixed SmartIcon, 71
floppy disks, *see* disks
fonts, 91-92, 120
footers, 100-101
:Format Lines command, 94
Formulas, 141
formulas, 49
   displaying, 54-55
   editing, 54
   entering, 50
   operators, 51
   parentheses, 52
   printing, 102
   recalculating, 66-67
functions, 52-53, 139-140

G

Go command, 99, 116
/Graph Options commands, 111
   Grid Clear, 113
   Legend, 111
   Titles, 109
   Save, 114
Graph command, 11, 106
Graph Legends & Titles dialog box, 111
Graphs, 142
graphs
   bar, 104-106
   creating, 103-107
   deleting, 107
   editing, 119-120
   enhancing, 109-120
   grid lines, 112-113
   HLCO, 104
   legends, 111-112
   line, 103
   mixed, 104
   naming, 113-114
   orientation, 120
   pie, 104, 107

   placement, 119
   printing, 115-120
   saving, 114
   settings, 107
   stacked-bar, 104
   titles, adding, 109-110
   XY, 103
grid lines, 112-113

H-I

headers, 100-101
Help, 10
HELP mode indicator, 7
HLCO graph, 104
Home (move cursor to beginning of line), 65
hyphen (–), 27
icons, 20-21
Icons program, 37
indicators, 34-35
Ins (change between INSERT and OVERTYPE modes), 64

J-K

key fields, 125-131
keyboard, 9

L

LABEL mode indicator, 7
Labels, 142
labels
   adding, 23-24
   aligning, 25, 81-85
   editing, 82
   entering, 23, 124
   prefixes, 81-82
   repeating, 84-85
   worksheets, 23-24
   prefixes, 81-82
Landscape, 142

161

LEARN status indicator, 8
legends, 111-112
Line command, 99
line graphs, 103
line heights, 93-94
Linking files, 142
list boxes, 17
List indicator, 34
lock key indicators, 7

M

Macro Library Manager program, 36, 142
Main menu, 11-13
MD (Make Directory) command, 154
MEM status indicator, 8
menu area, see control panel, 3
MENU mode indicator, 7
mixed graphs, 104
mode indicators, 6-7
mouse, 10
Move command, 11, 63

N-O

NAMES mode indicator, 7
Numeric formats, 70

one-key sort, 126
operators, 51
option buttons, 17
Options command, 99
Output range, 132, 136-137

P

page breaks, 100
Page command, 99, 117
palettes, 20-21
parentheses, 52
path, 15

pie graphs, 104, 107
POINT mode indicator, 7
pointing with mouse, 10
Print command, 11
Print menu command, 97-99
Print Settings dialog box, 99
PrintGraph menu, 116-117
PrintGraph menu command, 116
PrintGraph program, 115
printing
   graphs, 115-120
   ranges, 98
   screens, 100
   worksheets, 97-102
printouts, 118-120
programs
   add-in, 36-37
   Auditor add-in, 55-57
   BackSolver, 37
   Icons, 37
   Macro Library Manager, 36
   PrintGraph, 115
   Spreadsheet Auditor, 36
   Tutorial, 36
   Viewer, 36
   Wysiwyg (What-you-see-is-what-you-get), 36
prompts, 149

Q-R

Query Settings dialog box, 135
Quit command, 99

/Range commands
   Format, 69, 73
   Label, 82, 127
Range command, 11, 47, 99
range names, 47
ranges, 41-42
   deleting, 47-48
   deselecting, 45
   formatting, 69-72
   naming, 45-46

Index

pointing to, 44-45
printing, 98
selecting, 42-46
READY mode indicator, 3, 7
records, 122
   extracting, 136
   locating, 135
relative cell address, 58-60
REN (Rename) command, 157
right-justifying labels, 84
root directory, 154
rows
   adding, 86-88
   deleting, 88
   labels, 24

S

saving
   databases, 124
   files, 30-31
   graphs, 114
   worksheets, 27-31
screens
   printing, 100
   work area, 4-5
Settings command, 116-117
SETTINGS mode indicator, 7
Shift-Tab (move cursor five characters left), 9, 65
Size Manual Top command, 119
slash key (/), 3-4
SmartIcons, 144-148
Sort command, 128
Sort Settings dialog box, 127
sorting, 125-130
Spreadsheet Auditor program, 36
SST (step-by-step) status indicator, 8
stacked-bar graph, 104
STAT mode indicator, 7
status indicators
   CALC, 8
   CIRC, 8
   CMD, 8
   LEARN, 8
   Lotus 1-2-3, 8
   MEM, 8
   SST (step-by-step), 8
   STEP, 8
   UNDO, 8
STEP status indicator, 8

T

Tab, 9, 65
text
   borders, 94
   boxes, 17
   editing, 91-96
titles, 109-110
Titles command, 110
Tutorial program, 36
two-key sort, 129-130
type styles, 91-92

U-V

underscore (_), 27
Undo, 143
UNDO status indicator, 8, 35
VALUE mode indicator, 7
values, 25-26
Viewer add-in program, 36, 39, 143

W

WAIT mode indicator, 7
What-you-see-is-what-you-get, *see* Wysiwyg
work area, 4-5
Worksheet command, 11
worksheets, 49-51
   Averages column, 70
   columns, 86-88

163

creating, 22-24
formatting, 69-73
formulas, 52-55, 66
frames, 95
grids, 96
labels, 23-24
printing, 97-102
ranges, 41-48
retrieving, 32-35
rows, 86-88
saving, 27-31
values, 25-26
Wysiwyg (What-you-see-is-what-you-get), 143
  activating, 3, 92
  attaching, 89-91
  borders, 94
  deleting, 96
  fonts, 92
  line heights, 93-94
  menu, 92
  program, 36
  text, 91-96
  worksheets, 95-96

X-Z

XY graphs, 103